IN OTHER WORDS

Also by the Author

REBUILDING THE HOUSE

SINGING THE CITY:
  The Bonds of Home
    in an Industrial Landscape

IN OTHER WORDS

Tales of Paris and Language

LAURIE GRAHAM

WORD ASSOCIATION PUBLISHERS
Tarentum, Pennsylvania
2009

Copyright © 2009 Laurie Graham

The essays "Bibliophilia" and "L'Achat" first appeared in slightly different form in Creative Nonfiction Magazine. *The haiku quoted in "Bibliophilia" are from* An Introduction to Haiku, *by Harold G. Henderson, copyright* © *1958 by Harold G. Henderson. Used by permission of Doubleday, a division of Random House, Inc.*

Book design by Ruth Kolbert
Drawings by Linda Wallen

Library of Congress Cataloging-in-Publication Data

Graham, Laurie.
   In other words : tales of Paris and language / Laurie Graham.
   p. cm.
   Includes bibliographical references.
   ISBN 978-1-59571-370-4 (pbk. : alk. paper)
   1. Paris (France)--Description and travel. 2. Graham, Laurie. 3. Graham, Laurie--Homes and haunts--France--Paris. 4. Apartments--France--Paris. 5. Americans--France--Paris--Biography. 6. French language--Social aspects. 7. Paris (France)--Biography. 8. Pittsburgh (Pa.)--Biography. 9. Book editors--United States--Biography. I. Title.
   DC707.G685 2009
   070.5092--dc22
   [B]
                                                                                    2009012343

Contents

BIBLIOPHILIA *11*

L'ACHAT *30*

THE QUALITY OF THE LINE *55*

RES MEDICAE *80*

FITTING IN *104*

CONNECTIONS *124*

Notes 148
Bibliography 151

*But words are things; and a small drop of ink,
Falling, like dew, upon a thought, produces
That which makes thousands, perhaps millions, think.*
— Lord Byron, *Don Juan*

*[Words are] innocent, neutral, precise, standing
for this, describing that, meaning the other, so if
you look after them you can build bridges
across incomprehension and chaos.*
— Tom Stoppard, *The Real Thing*

*Les mots sont les passants mystérieux de l'âme.
(Words are the mysterious passers-by of the soul.)*
— Victor Hugo, *Les Contemplations*

BIBLIOPHILIA

THURSDAY, 2:30 P.M. THE MESSAGE ON THE answering machine comes in a rush. I recognize my mother-in-law's voice, but can decipher only the final three words: "BURNING. FIND BOB." Burning! What's burning? I must have just missed her call. I was away from the phone for only a moment. I dial Bob, my husband, on his pager. He is working the 3-to-11 shift at U.S. Steel. I fidget distractedly as I wait for the telephone to ring. When he calls, the first words out of his mouth are, "I already know."

"Know what?" I ask.

His sister has called. His house on the family farm is on fire. He is heading out there now.

"Should I come out too?" I ask.

"No. Wait till I see what the situation is."

Bob's four-year-old granddaughter, Caitlin, is spending the day with me. We settle down to wait, sitting cross-legged on the floor, piecing together her Scooby-Doo jigsaw puzzle. Still, lodged in the corner of my mind is the image of the long, steep driveway, the garage, and Bob's house in the small clearing on their tree-covered hillside.

Two hours later Bob calls again. He is standing in the front yard, facing the house, talking on his cell phone. He tells me that thirty fire trucks, manned by local volunteers, have formed a solid line up the driveway. It seems a preposterous number, but I don't quibble.

"The house is a total loss," he says. "The roof has caved in. The walls are still standing, but everything is burned inside." His voice betrays neither sadness nor alarm, only a heightened excitement.

Bob built the house with his own hands in the 1970s. Years later he and his wife divorced. His children are grown. He is not an expressive person. He will never put it into words. But I think of how he must feel, watching so much work, so much of his past go up in flames. It was the house his children grew up in.

I ask again, "Should I come out now?"

"No," he says. "There's nothing you can do. The firemen still won't let us inside."

I think of my books. Bob and I married later in life, each of us already established in our own places. Although we spent time in the house when we were first married, for the most part we live in my apartment now, in town. Bob has been thinking of selling the house. But many of my books, seven or eight bookcases full, are still there.

"The fire seems to have started in the living room," Bob says. "At one point the firemen thought they had it contained. But then it flared up through the walls into the attic, and it was hopeless."

I hear voices in the background, but I can't make out the words.

"They've managed to save some of your books," Bob says. "We're piling them in the garage. You can come out tomorrow and decide what's worth keeping."

I take Caitlin home to her parents, to Bob's son Jeff and his wife. I have told Caitlin that her daddy may be feeling sad about the house. When I leave them, she is snuggling up to Jeff on the couch, trying to cheer him up.

F*RIDAY MORNING*, 10 A.M. The sight is staggering. I have lived much of my life in books. Now to see so many, charred and sodden, strewn across the floor of the garage, heaped in plastic bags in hectic piles—it is too much for me. I can't take it in. My brain is too dull. I simply stand before them, my arms at my sides, looking. Where do I start? What can I possibly do? I feel a tightening in my throat. My first impulse is to give up, not even to try. I can't absorb the violation. I say to Bob, "Just throw them away."

"What?" he says.

"Just throw them away."

Bob ignores me—I know he thinks I will change my mind—and turns to show me the house. I turn to follow. There it stands, or what's left of it, its siding smeared black above the living room's picture window, the roof collapsed into the second floor. With the gabled end walls still standing, the roofline looks empty against the sky. I look up at the projecting end walls. The house is an American neocolonial and not an English mansion, but the devastation of the roofless walls makes me think of the jagged parapets of Thornfield Hall after the fire that blinded Mr. Rochester in *Jane Eyre*. If I were asked to sum up the look of the house in one word, the word that would come to mind is *forlorn*.

I follow the flagstone walk to the front door and step inside. My feet crunch through the loose bed of charcoal that covers the floor. The walls of the living room are an alien, inky black. They have the chipped, patterned shine of a coal mine. Although the fire has been out since yesterday evening, the smell of smoke still claws at my throat. Of one bookcase there is no trace at all. The books have been simply incinerated, vaporized. There is nothing left but empty space. It's as if they had never existed, as if no bookcase had ever stood there. Of another bookcase nothing remains but a bottom shelf of carbonized spines fused side by side in a bed of black. The cloth of the spines has burned away, revealing the charred backs of the books' signatures—the folded sheets that many books are composed of—still perfectly aligned. The third bookcase has become a thigh-high bank of charcoal, scattered with loose, singed pages. I can't bring myself to move closer, to learn what books they are from. The pages have survived better than the solid wood shelves that held them. Only the books have left a trace. No furniture remains.

    I follow Bob up the stairs to the second floor, tentatively, wondering if the treads will hold, feeling the crunch of charcoal with each step. The attic floor has collapsed under the weight of the roof, opening the black-walled stairwell to the sky. At the head of the stairs, the bathroom is chaos—all blackened drywall and attic debris heaped over toilet and sink. The frame of the mirror is an oval smudge fused to the once blue wall. Incongruously, a ruff of blue curtain hangs untouched across the top of the window.

    We make our way to the master bedroom in a sort of shuffle through the ceiling debris that forms a jagged layer over the carpet. Larger pieces of charcoal clunk against our shoes. In the bedroom doorway, a sheet of pink insulation drapes itself where it has fallen over the door. I can see from the doorway that the front wall of the room has burned off, opening it to the reach of yard beyond. The far side of the floor simply ends in thin air. It is an unnerving feeling, facing it. I feel momentarily unsafe, exposed, as if, even at this distance, I might fall over the edge. I look around the room, trying to take its measure. It seems so much smaller now against its backdrop of trees and sky. The wall was the path of the fire from living room to attic. Bob thinks there must have been a short circuit in the living room, but in what we'll never know for sure. I step forward, then back off from what seems like a softness under my foot, which I fear may be a weak spot in the floor.

I ask Bob, "Are we okay up here?"

He assures me that we are.

Bob is an engineer and knows a lot more about such things than I do. I decide to take his word that we are not going to plummet through the floor into the coal mine-like living room below.

Standing opposite the burned-off wall is an empty bookcase, still intact, and the bed, with sheets and blankets apparently unharmed. It is from the bookcases on the second floor that the firemen were able to rescue some of my books—desperate, I am told, to choose the most important ones but not knowing how to judge. I feel a rush of gratitude to these people who will risk their safety for someone they don't even know.

The smell on the second floor is of smoke turned putrid by partially burned carpet and the damp of the firefighters' water—a wet dog, stagnant sort of smell, but deeper and more malign. I reach into a closet and pull the filthy cleaners' plastic off a favorite, persimmon-colored blazer—stained now with a series of gray Rorschach blots that run vertically down the jacket front, arms, and lapels. It seems unlikely it could ever be cleaned.

Bob calls from the head of the stairs. "You have work to do," he says.

"What?"

"Start sorting through those books, decide which ones you want to keep. There are more in the barn."

I pull away from the closet, though not without noticing a

white, embroidered peasant blouse, tinged now in varied shades of grime.

Back in the garage, I see books lying on every horizontal surface, tool bench, windowsills, old tires, and of course the floor. The sight makes me feel almost frantic, and I take a deep breath to steel myself for the job at hand. I can bear the loss of the house, perhaps, selfishly, because it was never really mine. But the books are different—at least for me. Standing before them I don't know how to process the desecration of so many hard-won words. I don't know how to process the violation of so many books, that element of the sacred the very word book implies. I was brought up to revere books. I believe that words matter.

A mere glance reveals that these are mostly books that belonged to my family—works of Emerson, Robert Burns, Flaubert, the Brownings, Tolstoy, Voltaire, among others, many of them bound in soft green suede with gold medallions on the front covers. Scattered near the garage's open door is my grandfather's multivolume set of Sir Walter Scott. I kneel down and pick up one of the volumes, pocket-sized, bound in dark blue leather with gold stamping. The spine is burnt nearly through. I cradle the book in my hands, gently opening to its sodden pages that clump together as I riffle through. Inside the front cover, my grandmother has written: "Marcus W. Stoner, Xmas 1911." The set was her Christmas present to him over ninety years ago, five years before my mother was born. I run my fingers over the leather of the front cover, still so smooth and soft to the touch.

Near the Scott volumes is a pocket-sized, two-volume set of *The Count of Monte-Cristo,* with my father's bookplate, bound in maroon leather, part of Collins' New Universal Library, which was, I suppose, a sort of Modern Library of its day. At the time of its purchase, Universal Library books sold at a dollar a volume.

I also find schoolbooks of my mother's: Conrad's *The Shadow Line;* Whittier's *Snowbound and Other Poems;* Molière's *Le Malade Imaginaire;* a book of selected English essays—Bacon, Defoe, Addison and Steele, Fielding, Dr. Johnson, and more.

And yet it is my own schoolbooks that I gravitate toward, above all my French books, with my carefully inscribed lecture notes in the margins: Chateaubriand's *Atala* and *René*; hardcover editions of Flaubert's *Madame Bovary,* Balzac's *Le Père Goriot,* Zola's *Germinal,* published by Scribner's in its Modern Student's Library; a Garnier Frères edition of Baudelaire's *Les Fleurs du Mal.* All are blackened and smell of damp and fire. I gather them up and put them in the back of my Jeep.

With Bob's help I pull books from the plastic bags that the firemen had used to haul them, and lay them out singly on the garage floor to dry. As I reach in, water runs down the inside of the bags onto the backs of my hands. It is all I can do not to cry out at the horror of this cold, dripping water creeping into, seizing my books. I pull out a volume of George Bernard Shaw. The cloth is pushed upward on its boards like a wet, rumpled sheet. Some books are separated entirely from their bindings. I know I should do more, or I think I should. But I don't know what. And I am near the limits of my endurance. I select a few more books: a reprint of the 1900 edition of the *Guide Michelin,* "*Offert gracieusement aux Chauffeurs*"—offered free to drivers, and *Le Mécanicien Moderne,* published early in the last century in two oversized volumes with colored cutouts of the anatomy of early steam and internal combustion vehicles. Both belonged to my previous husband George Schieffelin, who died in 1988, an automobile collector and bibliophile whose wisdom and humor still enlarge my life. Recognizing shortly after we were married how much I loved his 1909 Stanley Steamer, he simply gave it to me—or rather sold it to me for a dollar. The bright-red, twenty-horsepower Model R roadster was the quintessence of verve and style, and I fired it up and drove it joyfully for years until donating it recently to a local car and carriage museum. I wasn't sure I would ever recover when George died. He had been the center of my life for nineteen years.

To George's automobile books I add the red leather copy of *The Book of Common Prayer* that I received at my confirmation and a *Color Source Book,* a book of color swatches organized according to origin: Chinese porcelain colors, Persian miniature colors, Japanese woodcut colors, the Adam greens, Giotto's palette, Turner's palette, the colors of Matisse, forty-eight palettes in all. The cleanness, the clarity of the colors remains untouched by the fire. Finally, I take two of the Scott volumes, the ones in the best condition, *Waverley* and *St. Ronan's Well.* But that's it. That's all I can do for now. I rub my blackened hands against my Levis. I'll confront the rest of the books in the garage on another day.

In the barn it is the same story all over again, books dumped hurriedly in tumbled stacks over much of the wide plank floor. I stand for a moment in the barn's dim light. A tiger cat darts behind the pyramid of hay bales that rises to the roof in one corner. These books too are charred and sodden. Some are already beginning to warp. Spines have burned off, or survive as scabby crusts. Many of the books are classics—Edith Wharton, Camus, Dreiser, Austen, Trollope, Virginia Woolf, Kafka. When I pick up Calvino's *If on a Winter's Night a Traveler,* the black of charcoal feels greasy on my hands. I lay each book down individually in what feels like a gesture of respect. There are spaces between the floorboards, and blades of hay broken off from the hay bales provide a sparse cover on which to place the books. It occurs to me that perhaps I should be stacking the books to keep them from warping and swelling. But then how would they ever dry? Two of the barn cats keep watch from the haystack as I work. One, a calico, is tucked to the side between

a hay bale and one of the roof trusses. The other, ginger and white, sits on his haunches at the top of the pyramid like some Egyptian god—above it all in all senses of the term.

When I finish, I stand in the doorway and look back at the scene. Gray light penetrates the spaces between the wallboards. Books cover most of the floor, lined up row after row. The scene resembles nothing so much as a morgue, and I just have to back away. It's been a long day.

MONDAY, 8 A.M. The insurance adjuster has driven here from his Connecticut headquarters to write up the damage to the house. Bob has told me that I must come up with a number, so I have counted the books in similar bookcases in town. The average number per bookcase, times seven bookcases, comes to 1,960 books.

The insurance company reimburses based on the number of books lost—not on provenance, memory, the worlds they open. I understand this. And we have no riders to cover books that are collectible or rare. In this calculation the older the book, the less valuable it is. It does not matter that nearly a hundred years ago my grandfather first held the Scott novels in his hands. What matters is Replacement Cost and Actual Cash Value, which the adjuster takes the time to explain to me. But I have trouble thinking of my books in terms of money.

The adjuster asks me to categorize the books according to binding and size. When he sees I have no ready answer, he proposes a breakdown of his own: 1,500 soft and hardcover books at an average price of $15; 400 large hardcover books at $25; 60 large hardcover books at $30. Quick mental arithmetic suggests a rather large sum. But that sum represents replacement cost. The actual cash value, which is what the policy covers, would be a fraction of that.

Standing with the adjuster on the flagstone walk, I notice

that one of the loose pages from the living room has drifted outside in the wind. It rests on an area of ivy and decorative stones that borders the walk. Its edges are singed, its corners rounded, and someone has stepped on it, leaving a muddy heel mark that smears into the white space above the text. Again I back off, afraid to know what book it is from. Knowing would make the loss too real.

While I was driving out to the farm this morning, I thought I was more in command than I was the other day, that I could handle the books with more dispassion. But when I return to the barn after talking to the insurance adjuster, there is the same sense of impotence and despair. I walk slowly among the books, picking one up, setting it down, picking up another: a first edition of Edith Wharton's *Madame de Treymes;* George Eliot's *Middlemarch;* an anthology of Chinese poetry called *The White Pony; An Existentialist Ethics* by Hazel Barnes, which I remember as a sort of Golden Rule dressed up in Existentialist-speak. I test the crackle of now-dried pages, gently cradle the burnt, cracked spines. A friend of mine, an archivist and bookwright, has told me that the best thing for water damage is to freeze the books to keep mold from developing. But I wonder if my books aren't beyond such remedies. I look over the scattered volumes of my Yale Shakespeare, small compact volumes bound in medium-blue cloth, which I have used so often to place a certain scene or line. The boards of many have warped as they dried. *Macbeth, Richard II, Henry IV, Parts I and II.* I think of John of Gaunt on his deathbed in *Richard II,* his paean to an England he now sees as compromised: "This royal throne of kings, this scept'red isle." I have been moved by the image of the wise and dying Gaunt since first reading the play in high school. The Yale Shakespeare was a gift from my mother. When she gave it to me she told me, "A complete set of Shakespeare is something everyone should have." Now the books lie on the hay like wounded birds, their boards like broken wings.

I gather a few more titles to take back to town: the Wharton first edition; my Modern Library set of the complete Greek tragedies; an anthology of haiku translated by Harold G. Henderson. I think of a poem by Matsuo Bashō that I have always particularly liked and page through the book until I find it. I notice that I have put a checkmark by the title "Clouds." Seeing it is like seeing an old and trusted friend.

> "Clouds come from time to time—
> and bring to men a chance to rest
> from looking at the moon."

I have often recalled the poem in bad times, the clouds that let you rest, the moments of darkness that shield you from the splendor of the light. On the previous page I see I have put a checkmark by another poem, "On the Mountain Pass":

> "Here on the mountain pass,
> somehow they draw one's heart so—
> violets in the grass."

The final line is almost mundane, and yet, set up as it is, the effect is exquisite.

To the books I have gathered already, I add F. Hopkinson Smith's *Charcoals of New and Old New York,* No. 97 in an edition of 125 copies printed on handmade paper in 1912. Born in Baltimore in 1838, Smith was a distinguished engineer, artist, and writer, who both wrote and did illustrations for *Scribner's Magazine.* Long after Smith's association with the company, I began work as a book editor at Scribner's and remained there for eighteen years.

Again, I gravitate toward books in French, my college edition of *Le Roman de Tristan et Iseut* and a leather-bound edition of *Acis et Galatée: Pastorale Héroïque en Musique*. On the endpaper facing the title page of the Acis and Galatea, someone has written in pencil *"Paroles de Campistron, Mises en Musique par Lulli"*—words by Campistron, set to music by Lully. The book commemorates the performance of the opera before *"Leurs Altesses Royales"*—their Royal Highnesses—at Lunéville on November 15, 1706. The *Acis et Galatée* and the Hopkinson Smith originally belonged to George. The link to Smith is that George was a member of the Scribner family, and himself a part of Scribner's.

I marvel at how books reveal the contours of a life—or in this case, parts of a number of lives—how one's passions, education, personal history are revealed in the books on one's shelves. So much of my life is spread out now at my feet. I wonder, too, what it is about the French books that makes them seem to me like touchstones, like a refuge. I leaf through the *Roman de Tristan et Iseut,* with its heavy stock and deckled edges, its ornamented initial caps at the chapter openings. The text is Joseph Bédier's rendering of the legend, and it calls itself *"un beau conte d'amour et de mort"*—a fine story of love and death. Although bound in paper, it has been scarcely affected by the fire. I feel drawn to it as if it were a talisman.

WEDNESDAY, 11 A.M. I have come out to the farm with my camera, hoping to capture the scene in the barn and the garage. A friend has urged me to write about the books, and although it doesn't address the problem of what to do about them, the idea has given me a sense of purpose. I focus in close-up on leather lifting off of boards, clumps of pages swollen as they dried, marbleized endpapers naked now with covers fallen away. I reposition a volume of Tolstoy on the hay-strewn floor of the barn to enhance the photographic effect. The front of its green suede binding, detached from the blackened spine, has writhed and shriveled from the pages under it. I will give the Tolstoy and many of the salvageable family books to my brother, who will want them for his two sons.

It occurs to me that I am achieving a certain distance now, though if I am, I am a little ashamed of it. Under the circumstances, even a degree of detachment feels unseemly. But I begin to realize that a certain toughness has been operating under my sense of loss. In choosing which books to take to town right away, I have chosen books associated with family, George's rare books, books I have interacted with in some profound way. Many of the books I treasure most, including my own modest collection of books on eighteenth- and nineteenth-century road building—an offshoot of my affection for the Stanley—are already in town. The classics are readily available. I think of what my archivist friend said to me in an e-mail: "If you want text, you can go to the library." I have known all along that, once Bob sold the house, I wouldn't have room for all of my books. Although I would have preferred a calmer—and less destructive—process of resolution, the fire has forced my hand. Still, it is one thing to contemplate simply throwing out so many books. It is another to actually do it.

Something else is beginning to nag at me. I want to know the source of the page by the flagstone walk. If the wind hasn't already blown it away. I can't entirely account for my change of heart, but not knowing which book it came from seems a gap in my knowledge now. I realize that if I don't find the page I will always wonder. As I approach the house, I peer hopefully toward the patch of decorative stones where it lay the last time I saw it. It seems unlikely that it could still be there. And yet, there it is. Still a little tentative, I look down and spot the running head under the page's singed top edge. It is set in small caps and it reads: "B I R D Y." The page is from *Birdy,* William Wharton's beautiful novel about a young man who becomes a bird.

I have lived a life largely forged by the imagination. Or rather, I have lived in worlds, places, created at least partly in my mind. I like to soak in, sink into auras. I often go to baseball games alone, absorbing the aura of the park, the rhythms and subtleties of each individual game. When I travel through my city, Pittsburgh, I travel not only through its topography but also through its story. Paris, where I have a tiny apartment on the Left Bank, is imbued with the language and literature I encountered long before I ever traveled there.

While still in school, I was immediately attracted to Baudelairean "spleen," to the self-obsessed melancholy of Chateaubriand's René, to Rimbaud's drug-assisted "derangement of the senses"—forms of alienation I thrilled to but would have been too risk-averse to act upon in my own life. I was equally drawn, perhaps even more so, to the limpid understanding of desire in Flaubert, the delineation of passion two centuries earlier in Racine. Above all, though, it was the language itself that attracted me. I remember as a child, kneeling at my mother's side, as she taught me the pursed-lip sound of the "u" in the French word *tu.* Again and again she pronounced the word as I repeated it until I got it right. People have asked what it is that so appeals to me about France, and I haven't been able to give more than superficial answers. But I wonder if language itself is a place—whether the sounds, the shape of a language are a sort of landscape that speaks to the soul. When you move from speaking one language to speaking another, you move to another place in your mind. Is that relevant?

I think of the beautiful sounds of the words: *heureuse, moine, soupir, pur, mémoire, matière, aurore.* The soft extension of the vowels, the exquisite extended "n" in *moine, fontaine.* The music of the language is in the gentle consonants, the lingering notes, the open endings of words. These are sounds to luxuriate in, like lying in a meadow or next to a stream. Comparatively unaccented, the music is elegant, not extravagant. *La langue coule*—the language flows.

I think of poem lines, or parts of poem lines, that I particularly like. From Lamartine's *Le Lac:* "*...et l'aurore/Va dissiper la nuit*"—and the dawn will dispel the night. The rising, expanding sound of *ore* in *aurore,* building like the dawn as the dissipating sound of *nuit* falls silent. From one of Baudelaire's *Spleen* poems: *"Pluviôse, irrité contre la ville entière"*—February, annoyed at the entire city. The grumbling, dreary sound of the word *Pluviôse*—the month of the Republican calendar running from late January to late February, derived from the word *pluvieux,* meaning rainy, wet. And then there is the frisson of the poem's grim last line: *"Causent sinistrement de leurs amours défunts"*—talk darkly of their dead love affairs. The word *défunt* deflates with a grunt. It just sounds dead.

I begin to think of the looks of words. One in particular persists in my mind: *étaient*—were, past imperfect, third person plural of the verb "to be." In my mind it looks like a mountain range. You could lie down, stretch out head to foot, between the "t"s. Then I think of a real visual onomatopoeia: *arête*. It just looks like a ridge, or crest. (It looks like a fishbone too, another meaning of the word *arête*. A *grande arête* is a fish's backbone.)

Of course onomatopoeia is not an exclusive province of the French, as anyone who has strolled along a babbling brook or traversed a ha-ha can attest. It may be that I feel French more keenly, that it seems to me to get to the core of things, because it is not my native tongue. I search for beautiful English words. When I was a child, a friend of my mother's used to tell me that the most beautiful expression in English is "cellar door." And wasn't it Henry James who maintained that it is "summer afternoon"? It occurs to me that, as in the case of "cellar door," the music of the word itself can draw the heart to the thing the word signifies. I myself am partial to the word *nevermore*. Here is one instance in which the music of the English far surpasses the French. Think of Poe's *The Raven* and possibly its most famous line: "Quoth the Raven, 'Nevermore.'" It has been translated into French as: *"Le corbeau dit: 'Jamais plus!'"* No comparison.

One of my favorite expressions in French is also mirrored in English: *"Détrompez-vous"*—don't kid yourself, set yourself straight. We have the same expression in English in the words *undeceive* and *disabuse*. But *undeceive* is a rather old-fashioned word, and *disabuse* derives from an archaic meaning of the word *abuse*. Another verb of the same type is the French *dépanner*—to repair, fix, from the French word *panne,* meaning breakdown. So the word literally means to un-breakdown— another charming double negative.

I wonder if it isn't, above all, the music of the language that has drawn my heart to French books, French things, the language itself—if French embodies the music of my soul. If the music of the word can draw one's heart to the thing the word signifies, does that explain why I feel so deeply the truths French words express?

With my camera tucked just inside the barn door, I pull out a few more titles to take with me: *La Cuisine est un jeu d'enfants*—Cooking is Child's Play, an oversized, illustrated cookbook with a handwritten preface by Jean Cocteau; *Georgia O'Keeffe: A Portrait by Alfred Stieglitz; Moments of Being,* a collection of autobiographical writings of Virginia Woolf; and *Book Decorations,* by Bertram Grosvenor Goodhue, published in 1931 in an edition of four hundred copies by New York's Grolier Club (a club of bibliophiles named for the distinguished French Renaissance collector Jean Grolier de Servières).

Goodhue was the architect of St. Thomas Church in New York and the National Academy of Sciences building in Washington, and designed buildings for the U.S. Military Academy at West Point. He was also the creator of Cheltenham type.

I stand back and look at the broad expanse of barn floor. Bob has ordered a Dumpster for the weekend, to dispose of the insulation and anything else in the house that he won't be able to burn. He wants me to throw out the books that I am not going to keep. I wonder if I will be able to do it, to hurl them into the Dumpster, just let them fly. So many are nearly gone in any case. But I don't know.

Another question is what I will do about the books I have saved. I have talked to a book restorer, and he tells me I can clean off the superficial blackening with alcohol. I could also have the more important books restored. To fix a fire-and-water-damaged book after it's dried, the restorer takes it physically apart—removes the binding, removes the stitching and unfolds the signatures—and washes the individual leaves in water and baking soda. Then he dries the signatures between weighted blotters, flattening the pages. Once dry, the signatures may be refolded and sewn back together. To save the binding, if it's in reasonably good condition, the warped boards are taken out and replaced by new ones. The price would be in the neighborhood of four hundred dollars per book. If I had put some of the books in a freezer, as my friend suggested, I could have taken them out one by one, and the restorer could have blown hot air with a heater fan on the fanned-out pages, then pressed them together hard with weights for three to four weeks.

But somehow I don't feel entirely comfortable with the idea of restoring the books. Cost aside, I can't help but feel that to restore them would be to deny a part of their history. The fire is a part of their story and that story warrants respect. And if a new binding were necessary, it would also mean a loss of authenticity, however degraded that authenticity may now be.

Bob will be tearing down the rest of the house himself, burning anything flammable in a bonfire behind the house. When he told me he wanted me to throw the books I'm not going to keep into the Dumpster, I asked him, "You mean you don't want to throw them into the fire?" Somehow the fire seemed cleaner and more respectful.

He looked at me over his shoulder as he walked back toward the house.

"No," he said. "That's not a good idea. Books are so hard to burn."

L'ACHAT

THE FIVE-HUNDRED FRANC NOTE WOULDN'T fit into the battered metal box. I could stuff it almost all the way through the slot, but it wouldn't drop. Visitors to the Église St-Sulpice filed by, and as I wrestled with the stubborn clump of paper, I felt the look of suspicion in what I imagined as their frugal French eyes. Five hundred francs! Almost a hundred dollars. Painted on the box in white were the words TRONC POUR PAUVRES DE LA PAROISSE—collection box for the parish poor. I folded the note again, into a fat little square the size of a postage stamp. I was here to express my gratitude, to seal the bond between me and this neighborhood, and equally compelling, to placate the demons who lie in wait to keep dreams from coming true.

Two days before, I had bought an apartment in the rue St-Sulpice. Only blocks from the church, the apartment represented the first chapter of a dream, a fixed point in a future whose direction I couldn't entirely see. I had quit my job of eighteen years as an editor in a New York publishing house. I was unsure of what would come next. Now, with the

L'ACHAT

apartment, I would spend at least part of my time in a culture I had always been drawn to and in a place where everything seems shinier because it has a new name.

It was my husband George who had put the idea into my head. Or perhaps it was there already and I just didn't know it. We were standing on the Pont des Arts, part of a group touring the Left Bank for prominent opera sites. Already that morning we had passed by no. 14, rue de l'Ancienne-Comédie, former site of the theater of the Comédie Française. The first act of *Adriana Lecouvreur* takes place in the theater's greenroom. At the point where the rue de l'Ancienne-Comédie meets the rue St-André-des-Arts at the carrefour de Buci, we found ourselves face to face with the angular café that inspired the Café Momus in *La Bohème*. (Equally memorable was the outdoor market nearby, a panoply of color and freshness, where stands lined the streets flush with plump fruits and vegetables, meats, and masses of flowers.) And standing by the fountain in the place St-Sulpice, we had looked up at the colonnades and arches, the uneven towers of St-Sulpice Church, imagining the seduction scene in Massenet's *Manon*, which is set in the church's sacristy. There was something deeply grounding in this blend of fact and fiction, of reality and story, of holding in my mind what I had seen on the stage of the Met and the real-world places that were part of its inspiration.

George was standing near the steps at the end of the Pont des Arts, framed by the magnificent dome and the curving arms of the Institut de France across the street. In his navy-blue suit and with his sweep of white hair, he seemed almost as elegant as his backdrop. Members of our group milled around us on the bridge. In a day or two we would be leaving for Provence. I turned to look back over the waters of the Seine, the rich architectural rhythms of the Louvre, the interplay of light and shadow under the soft July sun. "Paris, France is exciting and peaceful," Gertrude Stein wrote in *Paris France*—a more profound statement than it might first appear. I was sure I was at the center of the universe. I heard George's voice beside me. "Would you like to have an apartment here someday?" I looked at his face to see if he was serious. Where did that come from? We had never discussed anything of the sort. I answered yes almost reflexively, but I think it would never have occurred to me that I could do such an extraordinary thing. What did George know about me that I didn't even know myself? The French language had been something tacitly special in my family. In school I had been more drawn to French language and literature than to English. Did George see something in my eye? Who wouldn't regard Paris as some sort of transcendent ideal?

My first formal exposure to French was in nursery school or kindergarten. We would be perched on the floor on our long blue mats, the ones we also used for naps, as our teacher disappeared into a closet, then emerged with the big, round tray of porcelain animals. She would arrange herself on a stool, a stout grandmotherly presence in her dark print dress, then hold up each animal in turn. *Loup!* we would cry out as she held up the porcelain wolf, *ours!* as she held up the bear, *girafe! lion! tigre! éléphant!* We knew nothing of masculine versus feminine nouns, so the article probably never came into play.

I was blessed with my teachers over my school years: the French-born Madame McAllister, who turned all of our names into French equivalents, and deeming "Laure" too plain, dubbed me "Laurette." In her company it became a game to learn twenty vocabulary words a week. Then there were the sisters Marie and Annette de Saint Maurice, still French citizens, who shared their hopes with us, and widened our view of the world, as they spoke of sending in their absentee ballots in the referendum that would adopt the new French Constitution, drafted by Charles de Gaulle, to form the basis of the Fifth Republic. Still vivid in my mind is the image of Mademoiselle Annette, my teacher at the time, as she turned and gazed out the light-filled window at the front of the classroom. In her momentary silence, her hope for a new order and a better future for France, after the ineffectiveness and turmoil of the Fourth Republic, was an almost tangible presence.

But I had been to Paris only once before that first trip with George. On a serious budget. A girlfriend and I not long out of college. The trip was surely going to our heads as we deemed ourselves too sophisticated to visit the Eiffel Tower (well, maybe she was too sophisticated and I was willing to go along). Still, the thrill of being in Paris made even our hotel seem like an adventure. There is little new in its description: the sagging double bed that took up most of the room, the drab brown spread, the mottled velvet draping the window. A bathtub, a sink, and a bidet had been installed on a platform partially closed off by a makeshift wall. The communal toilet was in a curve of the staircase, a half-story down. It didn't take long to figure out that a bidet could be put to multiple uses.

The hotel was also the site of my first epiphany on French soil. On the morning after our arrival, at breakfast, at a small table in a hallway near the reception desk, I had my first *café au lait*—rich, chicory-flavored coffee made silken by the frothy, scalded milk. I looked down at my cup, almost unbelieving. I had never tasted anything as sublime. (I have since learned that one has *"café au lait"* at one's residence. When asking for it in a bistro, the term most often used is *"café crème,"* or simply *"crème."*)

More recently, as I felt myself pulling away from my publishing job, a friend of mine, who was taking lessons in conversation from a native French speaker, suggested that I do the same. Apart from answering a few letters in my capacity as editor in a publishing house, I had had little to do with France or the language since the trip with my Eiffel Tower-scorning friend. It was a good suggestion, as I had a pretty firm knowledge of French grammar, but I lacked the vocabulary and the facility of everyday conversation.

Tall and slender, *Monsieur le professeur* would arrive at our New York apartment, all ebullient charm, with a nearly permanent look of wide-eyed surprise. The opening ritual never varied. *Bonjour Madame! Bonjour Monsieur! Tout va bien? Oui, tout va bien, et vous? Oui, tout va bien.* Then perhaps a comment about the weather. The next words in the script, in a locution he had taught me, were mine: *"Vous voulez tomber votre veston?"* He would take off his brown tweed sport coat—we collaborated in the pretense that he would never think to strike such a note of informality if I hadn't suggested it—and hang it on the back of a chair, then head to the table by the window where for the next three hours we would chat. *Monsieur* had two passions: opera and food, or more particularly tenderloin of beef. Over a mid-lesson lunch of the latter, I could almost count on his suddenly leaping to his feet, with a swoop of his outstretched arms, to launch into some aria—he was partial to Verdi and Puccini—that happened to have come to mind, after which he would settle back down to his food. As the weeks and months passed, I found myself particularly fluent in vocabulary weighted toward theaters and the performing arts: *partition*—score, *répétition*—rehearsal, *salle comble*—sold out, *tête d'affiche*—top of the bill, *sur les planches*—on the boards, *bis!*—encore!, *étoile, vedette,* star—three words for star. And that is just the beginning. He also told me what an achievement it is for a popular singer to perform at the Olympia, the renowned music hall in Paris. I went at my lessons with uncommon zeal. It could be said that, at least in this instance, it took me a long time over the course of my life to wake up to what I really cared about.

L'ACHAT

And so the idea of buying an apartment in Paris took hold. I found myself urged on by friends, and by George, who had lived in Paris for a while in his early twenties. George loved women, and he loved me, and he applauded women who took off on adventures. Over the years, he had collected a number of Marie Laurencin lithographs, mostly of young women, lithe curly-headed creatures, some on horseback, delicately rendered but clearly masters of their fate. This may have been how he wanted to see me. Still, my idea/plan/dream was anything but fully formed. Although thrilled or, more accurately, dazzled (or perhaps because I was dazzled) at the prospect, I had only the vaguest notion of what I expected my apartment to look like. In my mind's eye, I saw one room, a brownish walled square, ill-lit, with a window high in one of the walls. Nor did I even quite know what I expected of it. At times, I imagined myself living in Paris, walking its streets, with new clothes to go with a new image, new hair. My apartment would be decorated with style and very French. Maybe I would write there. George was much older than I. His first wife had died. We had been married now for nearly seven years. I was his second wife. I knew that he wanted, while he was still here, to give me the gift of a richer life.

At the same time, there was reason to have doubts. Paris was far more a product of my imagination than of experience. I knew virtually no one there. And I knew nothing about Parisian real-estate practices, or the traps I might fall into. I had already been told that if I decided someday to sell the apartment, it was highly possible the French government wouldn't let me take the money back out. At one point I even said to George, "You know, sometimes the dream is enough. It doesn't have to come true." But that mood didn't last. Sometimes, out of nowhere, life just hands you a possibility that fits.

I started checking the real estate classifieds in *Le Figaro,* which is readily available in New York, turning immediately to

Ventes 6e ardt—Sales 6th *arrondissement,* or district. Although I didn't know what my apartment would look like, the streets I saw myself walking through—close, narrow, lined by the stucco façades of *vieilles maisons*—were those of the Sixth. (They were also the streets we had followed to the Buci market and the various opera sites the previous summer.) Long one of the intellectual centers of Paris, it had been frequented by writers from La Fontaine and Molière to Voltaire, the Encyclopedists, Balzac, George Sand, Beauvoir and Sartre, not to mention any number of American expatriates—Natalie Barney, Sylvia Beach, Hemingway, Eliot, Pound, and, of course, Gertrude Stein. The real-estate ads were anything but expansive. For a modest apartment, "*Odéon. 2 pièces, 45 m2, tt cft, charme,*" followed by a phone number and maybe a price would be typical. That is, Odéon area, 2 rooms, 45 square meters, all modern conveniences, charm. Unaccustomed to thinking in terms of square meters, I was soon on hands and knees, measuring our living room floor and then converting, in order to get some sense of what they were talking about.

My next step was to collect the names and telephone numbers of Parisian real-estate agents. I wrote to D. Féau, a leading Paris firm specializing in apartment sales, whose name was attached to many of the ads in *Le Figaro,* and got another name from the French stepfather of a friend. My best source was a New York agent, whose classified ad I had seen in a European travel magazine: "We specialize in the sale of apartments and other fine residential properties in Paris." I doubted that what my budget allowed for could be described as a "fine residential property," but I was soon armed with the names of a coterie of agents, all eager, I would discover, to impress the New York agent by being the one to find me the apartment I would actually buy.

My friend's stepfather had given me another tip: Paris

L'ACHAT

apartments were in such demand that once I found an apartment I liked, I would have to make up my mind about it within hours. "Once an apartment is advertised," he said, "thirty people will be at the door the next morning to see it." The corollary was that if I had to decide within hours, I'd have to have the requisite number of francs for the deposit readily at hand. A friend of mine, who had her own Paris dreams, had just opened an account through the Wall Street branch of Crédit Lyonnais. In response to my call to the bank, I soon received by mail a largely incomprehensible form, only part of which, fortunately, I was required to fill out. They also sent me an alphabetized list of their 160-plus branches in Paris, so that I could decide in which branch I wanted to locate my account. I chose the branch more or less blindly by its name: St-Germain-des-Prés. I sent off the form, a guaranteed signature, and a photocopy of my passport, as instructed, along with a check for an amount that I considered substantial, then waited for the bank's gracious letter of welcome. Instead, a few days later, I received a computer printout warning me about bad debts. I had already been told that if I bounced a check I might lose my banking privileges for a year. Still, I treasured this first concrete symbol of my future time in France. I had a bank account.

While immersed in these logistical details, I was becoming more and more drawn by Paris's mystical lure. I saw myself absorbed in a different sensibility—different sounds, different architectural styles. I dreamed of blending in, of becoming a new person in a new culture, if only from time to time. What an adventure it would be to become…French! My rational side was fully aware of how unlikely that was. Not long before, a French sales assistant in a dress shop near our apartment had informed me that I had an unmistakably "British" face. I was crushed. And I couldn't fool anyone for long once I opened my mouth. Nonetheless, I was determined to conduct the hunt for the apartment in French.

I telephoned two of the agents whose names I had been given from New York, shortly before we were to leave for Paris again. The first, to my surprise, was cheery, motherly—I was sure she had silver-blond hair pulled back from a smiling, middle-aged face. She couldn't wait to meet me. She would start on a list of possibilities right away. I reminded her of my budget requirements and she seemed unfazed. This came as a relief, as my friend's stepfather had warned me that I wouldn't find anything I could afford in the Sixth. Even the New York agent had backed off his initial assurances, asking me if I didn't want to consider looking in some other *arrondissement.*

The other agent, I could hear in her voice, had auburn hair, and was svelte and efficient and elegant. She was not an agent after all, but scheduled an itinerary of visits to apartments represented by agents, advised the client during negotiations, and helped with such chores as getting the electricity turned on and the phone installed. As we were to be in Paris for only two weeks, this seemed an ideal way to see a large number of apartments quickly and I agreed to her conditions and her fee. We would start the following Tuesday. Her name was Isabelle.

Although a little anxious about what lay ahead—I felt at times as though I were hurling myself headlong into the unknown—by the time we arrived in Paris, I was filled with the simple joy of being there. Everyone was beautiful and young. The sun always shone in the Luxembourg Gardens. Everyone was falling in love. It was a city of contrasts: the excited clack of women's heels along the pavement; the peaceful hush of the Jardin des Tuileries. And everywhere there were the words, French words, on storefronts, the sides of delivery vans, restaurants, brasseries, the blue-and-white street signs on the buildings' exterior walls: *pâtisserie, boulangerie, tabac, plomberie, fleuriste, livres anciens, gravures, avenue des Champs-*

L'ACHAT

Élysées, boulevard St-Germain, rue du Bac, Café de Flore.

Isabelle's hair was indeed auburn and she was efficient, but to my relief she was more cozy than svelte and elegant, and my forays with her formed the structure of my days. (George preferred to stay behind while I did the looking.) She also spoke English, which came in handy more than once in discussions of legal or structural detail, or when I simply got fed up with the effort of speaking French. It appeared that I could afford between thirty-five and fifty square meters in the Sixth, and the elements of shape, price, and size came together in almost infinite variety. I saw looming rectangular spaces, isosceles triangles, trapezoids, new moons. They could have been illustrations for a geometry textbook. Clearly, something had been made of every shred of each building's space. I felt tempted by a studio on the Seine, with five tall windows facing Notre Dame, but the room would soon be dominated by the kitchen being installed against the center of the interior wall, and you had to cross an unheated landing to get to the narrow, curving bathroom. There was also a great deal of traffic, both vehicular and tourist, along the *quai*. A sixth-floor *grenier,* or attic, not far from the Seine, had a view over the rooftops of Paris that was worthy of a postcard, but the shape of the apartment, a sort of boomerang, and the sloping outer walls arcing overhead were too unconventional for me to get my mind around. It also appeared that the building housed a number of American students. How could I dissolve into Frenchness if I were living with Americans?

Many of the apartments looked out not onto the street, but onto the quiet, often charming courtyards hidden behind the imposing closed doors of the buildings' façades. Most of the apartments had been renovated. The larger ones in my price range needed to be. To my surprise and disappointment—this was Paris, after all, the capital of taste and fashion—renovated bathrooms and kitchens tended to be gaudy. Some were even tiled in orange or purple. And the apartments had little in the way of architectural detail. I began to wonder if I would find anything at all. Was I being too particular? Or did I simply lack imagination?

I know I wasn't always, if ever, a vision of élan. Interspersed between my forays with Isabelle were visits with other agents to apartments not on Isabelle's list. The agent from D. Féau was red-haired, a little reserved, and, on the day that I met her, *très chic,* in a sleek skirt, high heels, and the requisite scarf tied just so. I guess she made me a little nervous. Sitting at a café between apartment visits, I managed to spill my Perrier all over her. She was convinced that, as an American, I would never be satisfied with an apartment in my stated price range. Americans wanted space, big rooms with high ceilings and parquet floors. I saw what I took to be French *volupté* incarnate in the most expensive of the apartments she showed me, where the owner lounged in a *luxe* of Chinese red—draperies, upholstery, carpet—under the aforementioned high ceilings. The large room's chief points of interest were its tall windows, a beautiful mantelpiece, and a fish tank filled with artificial pink coral. When I assured the agent that I couldn't afford the apartment, I think she lost interest in me. Or perhaps, in her defense, her agency simply didn't deal in properties as humble as the ones I could afford.

The miracle I was beginning to lose hope for appeared not in the Sixth but on the Île St-Louis. The Île is a place apart in Paris, quiet, self-contained, its narrow streets lined with seventeenth-century buildings and small shops. I had directions to find Madame C at her office in the rue St-Louis-en-l'Île, past the *chocolatier,* the *antiquaire.* As I approached I saw three women standing in the doorway of the agency. Madame C introduced herself and I replied earnestly, *"Je suis enchantée de*

L'ACHAT

faire votre connaissance." The three of them looked down at me, unable to quash a benevolent smirk. I knew I had said something slightly off, but I didn't know what until later, when I heard people saying *"enchanté de vous rencontrer,"* not *"faire votre connaissance,"* using *rencontrer* in a sense that was absolutely forbidden when I was in school. Then too, it could have been partly my schoolgirlish seriousness in reciting the entire formula, instead of merely responding *"Enchantée, Madame."* (At the opera one night, I watched a young woman being introduced to a man who was considerably older. She held out a languorous hand and deigned only a sort of growling *"Heureuse."*) I had recently had another lesson in linguistic outmoded-ness, when asking in a café for another croissant for George. *"Encore un croissant, s'il vous plaît,"* I said. *"Un autre croissant,"* the waitress corrected me, a much more natural usage for an English-speaker, but at one time not allowed—at least by my teachers.

Madame C punched the code into the *digicode,* the digital lock that is now a Paris commonplace. The big green wooden door clicked open into a large courtyard, at the far left corner of which was a small staircase leading to a studio on the *premier étage.* Madame C was clearly the most *sympathique* of the agents I would meet. *"J'aime bien le Wyoming,"* she told me—a statement I certainly hadn't anticipated—on our way from the agency to the apartment. She had vacationed there several times with her husband. She even suggested we have tea at her own apartment soon. She was proud of her new furniture and thought I might like it too.

We climbed the stairs to the studio and stepped inside. One by one the elements registered in my mind: fireplace, walls lined with bookshelves, large windows facing the courtyard, dark massive ceiling beams. The small bathroom and kitchen were tucked into a corner near the door. It was love at first sight.

This was a nest, a burrow, a place to curl up in. And it cost less than what I could afford! I imagined myself lying on my side on some sort of divan, head propped against my palm, with a multitude of throw pillows, reading a book. George would sit nearby in an upholstered chair, reading *Le Figaro* and the *Paris Herald*. In the evening we would go out for dinner, my heels clacking across the courtyard in the fading light.

And yet it wasn't until a couple of hours later, after a visit to another apartment with Isabelle, that the intensity of my attachment came into focus and I knew what I must do—now! I dashed into a nearby *brasserie,* dodging waiters and small square tables, and descended the winding staircase to the dimly lit *sous-sol.* There, between the doors to the *toilettes,* under a single yellow light was the pay phone. I sat down on the dark, varnished stool and, fumbling with my address book and coins, reached the agency, though Madame C was not there. Madame C's colleague assured me she would pass on my offer to the owner's agent right away. I headed back to George in a flurry of exhilaration and agitation.

I could hardly sit still, alternately exclaiming over the apartment and agonizing over whether I'd made the offer in time. Seventeenth-century building! Beams! Bookshelves! Fireplace! Charm! But what if I was too late? I should have made the offer right away! I hope I got there in time! So peaceful, quiet! Such character! Courtyard! Windows! Oh, if only! George just listened, amused. When the phone rang, I froze for a moment before picking up the receiver. It was Madame C's colleague, *désolée.* A young man had seen the apartment right after I did and had made an offer on the spot. As I was exclaiming to George, the young man was signing the contract. I had made up my mind about the apartment within hours, but it hadn't been good enough.

So it was that when I saw the apartment in the rue St-Sulpice

L'ACHAT

I pounced. It was a favor, really, to another agent to fit it in before my appointment with Isabelle at three. I didn't want to see it. I had been told that it had two rooms, living room and bedroom. But as the entire apartment totaled only forty-three square meters, they could only be two *small* rooms. And besides, how could I live anywhere but the Île St-Louis? I saw myself shopping in the small market off the rue St-Louis-en-l'Île, whose jovial, white-aproned proprietor held court from behind a broad display case of cheeses. I thought of the mimes, like pencil-thin mechanical dolls, behind Notre Dame on the Pont St-Louis. I pined for the warmth of the apartment I had lost, the solidity of those dark, massive beams.

I met the agent at 2:15 in a sleek glass building in the rue Bonaparte. Raymond was a tall slender man with black hair, whose legs seemed to account for at least two thirds of his six foot-plus frame. As we made our way to the apartment, past shop fronts and the stucco façades of old houses, I clambered after him, nearly slipping on the drizzle-slicked sidewalk. The hem of my narrow French skirt tugged at my knees as I struggled to match his stride. Most of the time he was a half-stride ahead, offering a running commentary over his shoulder, only some of which I took in. I was beginning to feel like a foolish American, more than a half-step behind the old world. Without warning, he wheeled into the vestibule of a house near the head of the street. The neighborhood seemed attractive, but I barely saw it as I leapt after him and we were buzzed inside.

"Don't worry about the stairwell," he hailed as we started up the winding staircase to the *troisième étage* (the fourth floor according to American calculation). "The repairs have already been voted." Voted by the owners of the apartments in the building, that is, so that the cost to the apartment I was to see would be paid by the current owner. The staircase was, as the French say, *en travaux,* under repair, though what I noticed

43

more was the beauty of its lines, the burnished wooden steps, the wooden handrail on what I took to be wrought-iron balusters circling upward from floor to floor.

The door to the apartment was open as we reached the landing of the *troisième étage*, and I could see immediately the graceful carved stone fireplace in the living room, and above it a huge rectangular mirror reaching nearly to the ceiling. Large casement windows, somewhat crooked with age, looked out on a row of houses that could have been a stage set for *La Bohème*. The apartment had a living room, with alcove, and a bedroom. The rooms were small, but the layout made maximum use of space. The kitchen and bathroom had been renovated in muted earth tones and white. There was even a window in the kitchen. I hardly noticed the slope of the living-room floor, which for me was simply another indication of the building's venerable history. I felt almost immediately at home, astonished that I had found something that could make me almost forget the Île St-Louis.

Back in the street, eyes lowered, I could feel the words in my throat. But no matter how hard they pushed, I couldn't get them out. Raymond strode on, uncharacteristically silent. Should I? Should I wait? I wanted to, but…oh, I didn't know. All of a sudden the step seemed immense. Should I keep on looking? What if there's another apartment I'd like even better? From the whirl of indecision the words finally burst out: *"Je vais faire l'offre"*—I'm going to make an offer. We walked on. I'd done it. I felt a little dizzy, elation thinly edged with anxiety. When we reached the office, I learned that this time no one else had gotten there ahead of me. I was still a little giddy, but managed to settle down enough to sign the *offre d'achat,* which was to be accompanied by ten percent of the purchase price. They had to teach me how to write a French check.

I arrived in the rue du Bac a half-hour late, to find Isabelle and Madame R, yet another real-estate agent, waiting for me.

I managed to convey to Isabelle under my breath that I had just made an offer on another apartment. We decided not to disappoint Madame R, who after all had been waiting for me for over half an hour. We would look at the apartment here as if nothing were amiss. Unfortunately, it would not be without leaving one flank exposed. On our return to the street, Madame R found a parking ticket on her windshield. *Oh là là!* She chased after the policeman, exclaiming over the injustice of it all. She was only doing her job, she wailed, how could it be helped, there were so many cars in Paris, she had to make a living, she'd been parked there for only a moment, where was his sense of fair play, she was an honest, hard-working citizen, why wasn't he out chasing criminals? "If you'll write a letter detailing your complaint…," the policeman proposed, then drove off. More exclamations as to the injustice of it all. Isabelle gestured helplessly. Shopkeepers came out to sympathize. "If only you'd left the key with me," one of them cried. I felt as though I'd stumbled into an *opéra bouffe*.

It was a performance I knew I would never be able to replicate. Granted, I was not a tourist anymore. I owned an apartment here, almost. Already that set me apart from the many visitors who, much as they loved the city, were merely passing through. I belonged here in a sense that they did not. I said goodbye to Isabelle and Madame R, and strolled up the rue du Bac toward the flood of traffic in the boulevard St-Germain. But would I ever become a real part of this city? Would the city ever embrace me? Would I ever be able to dissolve into Frenchness? I felt an extraordinary calm. Did it matter? Could I not simply take what the city had to give? Could I not simply relish the joy of being in this beautiful place? I wondered if one ever came to take all this for granted. If you were born here, grew up here, led your daily life here, did you see it fresh? Or do the preoccupations of daily life largely blind you to your

L'ACHAT

physical surroundings? What is it like to have such beauty as the locus of your life?

In France a buyer makes an offer, that is, signs an *offre d'achat* and hands over a percentage of the purchase price, and then has time to repent. Five days or so after signing the offer sheet, he is expected to appear before a *notaire* to sign the *promesse d'achat,* which makes the sale binding. Until that time the buyer may change his mind and his check will be returned. If he changes his mind after signing the *promesse d'achat,* he forfeits his hand money. At least that's how it was laid out to me.

I invited two American friends to meet George and me at the apartment at 2:00 p.m. the following afternoon. George and I were the first to arrive, after picking up a key at the agent's office. As George paid the driver, I got out of the taxi and had my first real glimpse of the neighborhood I had seen only in a whir the day before. The narrow streets were lined with five- or six-story houses, almost all with shops at street level, and wrought-iron *grilles,* or railings, and geranium-filled window boxes on the floors above. Most, if not all, of the buildings were presumably divided into apartments, just as mine was. Superstitiously, I delayed looking directly at my own building. What if I'd made a mistake? If I had, I couldn't quite bring myself to know it. When, finally, I turned and looked up at the building's façade, I could only stare. Oh, my God.

It seemed to be disintegrating. It was mottled with damp, riddled with crevasses and peelings. One of the shops was boarded up. And there was an ominous bulge between the first and second floors. It was without question the ugliest, most decrepit-looking building on the block. Was this why Raymond had walked so fast? So that I wouldn't see? The gears of a bus ground menacingly from around the corner. What have I done? I asked myself. What have I done?

Gail and Pat arrived and immediately dismissed my anxiety.

"It's only the stucco," Pat assured me. Gail agreed. Apparently, the façade of a house like mine would be built of stone with an overlying layer of stucco, which was not integral to the building's soundness. Once in the apartment, I felt the delight I had felt the day before. Light poured in through the windows. Gail and Pat went from room to room exclaiming over the apartment's charm. George, on the other hand, stood in the living room dismayed, struggling to see what I saw in it. I said nothing. I opened one of the windows, only to hear the roar of another bus. Yikes. But once the window was closed, it was quieter. "After you've been here a while," Gail said, "you won't notice the noise." And indeed I did seem to forget it after a few minutes. I took photographs and measured every wall and nook with my metric tape measure. I knew George liked things that impressed. It would take him a while to understand the lure of this cleaned-up *vie de bohème.*

A subsequent stroll through the neighborhood was breathtaking. The apartment was only blocks from the boulevard St-Germain, the place de l'Odéon and the Odéon Theater, the Luxembourg Gardens, and of course St-Sulpice Church. Along the streets, specialty shops alternated with rare book and print dealers, publishers. Crayfish and oysters lay on beds of ice in restaurant windows. *Boulangerie, pâtisserie, charcuterie, pharmacie*—those words again—were only steps from the apartment. And the bank branch I had chosen? That, too, was only blocks away in the rue de Rennes. I couldn't get over the coincidence. Perhaps I was meant to be here after all.

Still, visions of my building's degraded façade haunted me through the night. At 4:00 a.m. I lay awake, eyes wide in the darkness. George slept peacefully beside me. Anxiety had curled into my gut. How could anything so decrepit-looking be sound? I knew I could get out of the sale if I needed to. I hadn't yet signed the *promesse d'achat.* But I didn't want to get out of

it. I felt already invested there, unable to pull away.

The next step was to talk to the *syndic,* one of the many professional administrators who handle the affairs of Paris apartment buildings. It was he who would give me a copy of the *procès-verbal* of the most recent *assemblée générale,* that is, the minutes of the most recent meeting of proprietors of apartments in the building, and he who would tell me about the condition of the building. "Not at all," he chuckled, when I spoke of my concerns. "The building is not *délabré*"--beyond repair. It had recently been replumbed and rewired, a new security system had just been installed, and the *ravalement*—the repair of the façade which by law was to be done every twelve years—was projected. (As it had not been voted, I would be the one to pay for my apartment's share if I decided to buy.) Isabelle had instructed me to ask if the shop was boarded up because of legal proceedings, which in France are not uncommon and can be little short of Dickensian. But no, the shop was *en travaux*—in this case meaning undergoing alterations, and would open in the spring. The next *assemblée générale* would take place in less than two months.

It certainly sounded good. More than good. Did I dare just be happy? Why was I being so hesitant? Had I been trying to make judgments through too-American eyes? What kind of promise had I been expecting? Nothing is risk-free. I decided to follow my heart. The various legal and title searches had already been done, which meant that I would not have to wait the usual one to three months between signing the *promesse d'achat* and the final sale. I had already called my bank in New York to ask them to wire the funds I needed to my Paris account. George was in the room when I called. As I recited account and telex numbers, he interrupted to tell me they should take half the money out of his account. His tangible support seemed like the ultimate seal of approval.

L'ACHAT

Maître V, the *notaire,* was a robust, cheerful man in a gray tweed suit, who had come in from his office in Trouville for the closing. (I didn't ask why we were using a *notaire* from Trouville instead of one of the many who surely existed in Paris.) He opened the proceedings by explaining that he had a slipped disc, then throughout the meeting squirmed and winced self-mockingly with each twinge in his back. He had an appointment with his chiropractor at 6:30 that evening. He looked out over the desk at the real-estate agency at me, Raymond, and Raymond's English-speaking colleague. The seller, having given power of attorney to the *notaire,* was not present. Nor were there any lawyers.

Maître V read dutifully from the myriad documents arrayed on his desk. At my request, he showed me the *D.I.A.,* the *Déclaration d'Intention d'Aliéner,* which someone, probably Isabelle, had told me to ask about. But having no idea what it was, I could only nod when he held it up. (Isabelle had neglected to tell me what it was about it that I was supposed to be watching for, and I had been so busy taking notes that I hadn't thought to ask.) He also assured me that the building's *État Hypothécaire* was less than two months old and *"vierge," "sans exercice,"* as Isabelle had said it should be, though I wasn't entirely sure what those terms signified. It occurred to me that I was, perhaps unwisely, throwing caution to the wind, but I decided that any country so strict about checking accounts would probably be equally unforgiving of any *notaire*-related hanky-panky. And besides, I had Raymond and his colleague with me, eager to please the agent in New York. I handed over a bank check for the sale price, plus a separate check for the *notaire's* customary ten percent, most of which goes to the state. (In one note of caution, I had gotten an *attestation* from the bank to the effect that the funds had originally come from abroad. That would presumably ensure my being able to take the money out of France should I sell the apartment someday.) My original check for the hand money was returned and I emerged from the meeting with an aged-looking document detailing the previous owners of the building and the rules of the subsequent co-proprietorship (I was told not to lose the document on pain of death), an *attestation de propriété* stating that I had bought lots 9, 10, and 11 in the building, and a fat, stubby key. The *acte de vente*—the deed—would arrive in six months.

So, I was a homeowner. I walked slowly back to the apartment and sat cross-legged in front of the fireplace. There was something so pure, so peaceful in the gray stone of the mantel poised against the white wall. I reached for the "aged" document, page after typewritten page, bound in heavier gray stock, which had actually been prepared in 1949 with the establishment of the co-proprietorship. I was a part of this now. Wherever the records were kept, I would be listed as one in the sequence of the building's owners. Over history, from the seventeenth century, when the building was constructed, to some unknown date in the future, my name would be one of the series of names, some of which came before mine and others that came after. I visualized the names flowing down a sort of unfolding scroll. In this way at least I would belong to the city. As long as there was a Paris, my name would be a part of it.

Standing by the poor box at St-Sulpice, I was secluded from the bustle suddenly resonating at the back of the church. I squeezed hard on the folded banknote, pressing each edge. A wedding or some other religious celebration would begin soon. Four young boys in short pants, with navy-blue bows at their collars, and four young girls in white dresses busied themselves in anticipation, lining up, tugging at their clothes, scarcely succeeding in keeping their voices low. I pushed one edge of the folded banknote into the slot in the poor box, forcing it

L'ACHAT

through incrementally until it dropped. Superstition aside, my offering was, most profoundly, a symbolic gesture of the heart, of commitment to the neighborhood, and a quiet message, "I am here." I glanced back at the nave, the series of chapels along the far wall. In an exception to my usual response to Paris structures, the beauty of the church's massive interior, if indeed it was beautiful, was not immediately apparent to me. But perhaps time would give me a more discerning eye. I looked down at my watch. George would be waiting for me. I turned and left the dimly-lighted church and walked out into the sun.

THE QUALITY OF THE LINE

For a long time after I bought my Paris apartment, I would walk the streets of my neighborhood looking for bulges in the buildings' façades. Passing house after house, hewing to the sidewalk in deference to passing cars, I would proceed through the narrow, centuries-old streets, craning my neck, peering upward to gauge the line of each house front, pausing from time to time, thinking, hoping that here, possibly, was a house that deviated from the perpendicular. At times I would find façades cracked and mottled with damp, even perhaps with a slight bulge at the edge, or at least what could conceivably be described as a slope. I would linger before the façade, peering, squinting, trying to conjure it into qualifying. But I would finish disappointed. I could find nothing to resemble the undeniable bulge of my own building's *premier étage*.

My building had been constructed in the mid-seventeenth century as a small hotel. Its simple façade was devoid of decorative detail and the *grilles* at the windows were more intersecting straight lines than adornment. Inside, and equally simple, the burnished chestnut steps of the circular staircase and the varnished cherry banister on its slender metal balusters testified to the building's age. *Châtaignier,* chestnut. *Merisier,* wild cherry. Centuries of footfalls had rounded the forward edges of the stair treads; the pull of countless hands had separated joints in the handrail. I had not been hoodwinked about the bulge. I was aware of it before I bought the apartment, which was, at forty-three square meters, the larger of two on the third of five floors. "To act on impulse is one of the secrets of happiness here," the art critic John Russell wrote about Paris. Perhaps I hadn't acted on impulse in buying the apartment, but on a corollary, faith. I knew that the building had recently been replumbed and rewired, and my own apartment entirely renovated, while retaining its old casement windows and its original stone fireplace. I had been assured that the building was sound. And why, indeed, would owners re-plumb and rewire a building that wasn't? Still, I wanted the reassurance of finding another building that had a bulge.

George's gift of the apartment had been a gift more of possibility than of money, though in fact he had given me half the sum I paid for it. At the time, I was vague about what direction my life would take, having quit my job at Scribner's, the New York publishing house that had been founded by his great-grandfather. George was much older than I was. He knew how deeply I felt the French language, how profoundly seated it was in my makeup, though I'm not sure I was always aware of it myself—I had experienced it for the most part only in school. (One clue may have been during the first night we spent together, when in response to something he said I blurted out a line from Baudelaire.) George was of a generation and a social world that regarded Paris as fundamental to one's completion as a person. In proposing that I buy an apartment in Paris, he was suggesting something that, to him, was not extra-

THE QUALITY OF THE LINE

ordinary, much as it was so to me. But he was also showing me that I could open up that French part of myself, that my life could contain something larger even than New York.

Though there is no such official determination, I had an implicit sense of my neighborhood's borders: to the north, the boulevard St-Germain; to the west, the place St-Sulpice; to the east, the rue Monsieur-le-Prince, or perhaps by extension, the rue de l'École-de-Médecine; and to the south, the rue de Vaugirard and the Luxembourg Gardens. It is a neighborhood full of life, of the present, of accommodations to the present. At a tiny restaurant, at the foot of the rue de Condé and the rue des Quatre-Vents (so named for the sign whose *"têtes d'amour"* once blew toward the four cardinal points), diminutive round tables with white linen tablecloths and small pots of violet-like *campanules* spill onto the sidewalk. Standing pots of red camellias artfully placed amid the tables anchor the scene and give it style. In the rue des Quatre-Vents, at a grocery with less space than my apartment, the proprietor lifts a section of floor, props it up, and descends the ladder-like steps deep into the basement to replenish his stock of Evian water. A young man in pantaloons strides up the rue de Seine in time with the tune he plays on his harmonica. A terrier out for a stroll with his elderly, tweed-coated master, grabs the end of a street sweeper's broom and tugs at it mightily as water flows by in the gutter. The street sweeper laughs as passersby pause, smiling.

Walking its streets, I took the neighborhood into my bones. Most of its eastern half had been vineyards before my street, or that part of it east of the rue de Tournon, was created in 1501. Only steps from my apartment, the street abuts the rue de Condé, which was cut through around 1520, though it didn't acquire its current name until 1612, when the Hôtel de Gondi was bought by Henri II, prince de Condé, duc de Bourbon, d'Enghien et de Châteauroux, descendant of Robert de France (the sixth son of Saint Louis), cousin of Henri IV, prince of the blood and longtime heir presumptive to the Crown. Whew. The large house, described by a contemporary as "not unworthy of a prince of the blood," was magnificently furnished and surrounded by vast reaches of garden. Five Condés succeeded Henri II as owners, including Louis II, Prince de Condé, a military general of shifting loyalties known as the Great Condé, until Louis-Joseph abandoned the house in 1764. Presumably, he did not leave the house because he was down on his luck. He had just acquired the Palais Bourbon.

The lives of untold numbers of aristocrats, revolutionaries, and literary lions have unfolded in my neighborhood. In 1773 the king, Louis XV, bought the Condé property from Louis-Joseph for 4,168,107 *livres* and 15 *sols* and ordered it razed. He had in mind an entirely new quarter, at the center of which would be a new home for the Comédiens du Roi, more familiar to us as the Comédie-Française. Opened nine years later, and inaugurated by Marie-Antoinette, the classically-inspired theater, which crowns the regal ascent of the rue de l'Odéon, stands on what was once the lawns and trees of the Condé *jardin en terrasse.*

I didn't look long for bulges in the rue de l'Odéon. The street was a latecomer, opened in 1779 as the central approach to the theater. Its buildings are of greater standing than mine, wider, of more noble aspect, with courtyards entered from the street through wide, tall green doors. Differing only in decorative details—balustrades, *grilles,* cornices—the buildings' façades maintain a height and regularity of line that sweep the eye to the columned theater at the top of the slope. It is a street of elegant galleries, rare book and print shops, even a shop offering silk *passementerie* handbags and a *Maison de Théières,* displaying rows and rows of teapots, predominantly oriental, on cloth-covered risers in the window. Only two storefronts at

THE QUALITY OF THE LINE

the beginning of the street, old, wooden, one cream-colored, the other brown, under a green and white striped awning, recall the rue de l'Odéon of Adrienne Monnier and Sylvia Beach.

In a photograph taken by Gisèle Freund in 1938, three years before he died, Adrienne Monnier and James Joyce stroll side by side up the rue de l'Odéon. Monnier, pleasantly stout, wears a full, ankle-length skirt, a vest, and a long-sleeved white blouse with a round collar. Joyce, his felt hat tipped up to his hairline, is dressed in a suit and tweed overcoat, an umbrella hooked over his arm. Unassuming metal signs, hanging from wrought-iron brackets on the storefronts, read *"Tailleur,"* tailor, *"Fourrures,"* furs. The area is no longer, as Monnier called it, *"Odéonie"*—Odéonia, or, as Joyce dubbed it, "Stratford-on-Odéon." Monnier's *La Maison des Amis du Livre*, a lending library as well as a bookshop, no longer exists at No. 7. At No.12, all that remains of Sylvia Beach's Shakespeare and Company is a plaque that reads:

En 1922
Dans Cette Maison
Melle *Sylvia Beach publia*
"Ulysses"
de James Joyce

When Beach moved into No.12, the shop was flanked by shoemakers, a corset maker, and a nose-spray manufacturer. (The nearby building at 8, rue de Dupuytren, the first site of Shakespeare and Company, now houses a unisex hair salon and an aromatherapy boutique.) It was the combined genius of Adrienne Monnier, a French Catholic, and Sylvia Beach, an American Presbyterian, that made the rue de l'Odéon a center of both French and expatriate literary life between the two world wars. Sherwood Anderson, Stephen St. Vincent Benét,

Léon-Paul Fargue, Ernest Hemingway, Paul Valéry, André Gide, Jules Romains, Gertrude and Leo Stein, Simone de Beauvoir, André Breton, and Marianne Moore were among the many whose paths crossed here. At 8, rue de l'Odéon Robert McAlmon's Contact Editions published work by William Carlos Williams, Hemingway, and Gertrude Stein. All partook of the "atmosphere of spiritual effort" that Joyce attributed to Paris, that idealization of the creative that spurs the artist to strive for the unattainable. Beach and Monnier lived together at 18, rue de l'Odéon for seventeen years, until Beach found herself supplanted in Monnier's affections by the photographer Gisèle Freund, and the union between the long-time lovers, though not their professional relationship, came to an end.

I feel more ambivalent about another theme in the history of my neighborhood, and it occurs to me that my responses may be influenced by reading done years ago that has nestled into my subconscious. On the same street, at 10, rue de l'Odéon, there is another plaque:

Thomas Paine
1737-1809
Anglais de naissance
Américain d'adoption
Français par décret
a vécu dans cet immeuble de 1797 à 1802

(Thomas Paine, 1737-1809, English by birth, American by adoption, French by decree, lived in this building from 1797 to 1802.) The plaque goes on: *"Il mit sa passion de la liberté au service de la Révolution française, fut député à la Convention et écrivit* Les Droits de l'Homme"—He put his passion for liberty to the service of the French Revolution, was deputy to the Convention, and wrote *The Rights of Man*. Written in response to

THE QUALITY OF THE LINE

Edmund Burke's *Reflections on the French Revolution,* Paine's two-part pamphlet made him a hero in France (and persona non grata in England). He was made an honorary citizen and was elected to the National Convention, the constitutional and legislative assembly that sat from September 1792 to October 1795. As an American, I learned to revere Thomas Paine for his role in the American War of Independence, his pamphlet *Common Sense.* And yet, when I think of the French Revolution, I think less of heroes than of blood.

Around the corner from my apartment, on the site where Danton's house once stood, a huge, bronze statue of the revolutionary leader looms high on a pedestal, surging with life—a figure uncannily reminiscent of Rodin's *Balzac.* Opposite the statue, across the boulevard St-Germain, one enters a courtyard, where, in 1790, in a loft, Dr. Guillotin made the final adjustments on his "philanthropic decapitating machine." Jean Paul Marat lived, and died, at 20, rue de l'École-de-Médecine, stabbed in his bath by Girondist sympathizer Charlotte Corday. Eventually, both Danton and Corday became subject to the philanthropy of Dr. Guillotin's machine. Paine himself narrowly escaped execution by the same means, when he was imprisoned and sentenced to death by Robespierre for opposing the execution of Louis XVI.

The blood shed in the French Revolution has been personalized in a way that the blood of the American Revolution has not. Danton, Marat, Louis XVI, Marie Antoinette, the Carmelite nuns. With the French Revolution, too, there are the mobs and the ghoulishness of the means of execution. But for me, all of it coalesces in the figure of Madame Defarge in Dickens' *A Tale of Two Cities,* encoding into her knitting the names of aristocrats and other "enemies of the Revolution." It is in part her grisly pleasure, her furied knitting as heads dropped on the scaffold, that is the origin of my unease.

The blood of the barricades. You still see it today in France in the frequent strikes and in the many demonstrations, some of them charming, more of them not. I could hardly believe my eyes one summer as I approached the Champs-Élysées from the place de la Concorde. It seemed to be entirely absent of cars, and crowds of spectators milled along the borders of some sort of grass. I have a newspaper photo of the avenue that day, entirely covered in flats of wheat brought in from the countryside by farmers. From the Rond Point to the Arc de Triomphe, they had "brought the country to the city," and transformed the avenue into a field of wheat—an incongruity that engendered delight. But later that summer, their methods became, as the newspaper *Le Figaro* phrased it, more *"regrettable,"* with the poisoning of ninety-four sheep shipped in from England, and the burning alive of two hundred more.

The language itself is not exempt. In his *Histoire du Romantisme,* Théophile Gautier described *"La Bataille d'Hernani,"* the tumult that broke out at the Comédie-Française between the supporters of Victor Hugo and the defenders of classicism over the first two lines of Hugo's *Hernani:*

> *"Serait-ce déjà lui? C'est bien à l'escalier Dérobé."*

(Could that be him already? It [the knock] did come from the secret staircase.) Hoots, jeers, howls of protest erupted in the audience, a prelude to the fisticuffs to come. Classicists were scandalized by *"Ce mot [Dérobé] rejeté sans façon à l'autre vers"*—this word tossed unceremoniously to the next line, breaking one of the classic rules of French versification. They abhorred *"cet enjambement audacieux, impertinent même"*—this audacious, even impertinent enjambment. Enjambment? They went nuts over an enjambment? Webster's—**"enjambment:**

THE QUALITY OF THE LINE

continuation in prosody of the sense in a phrase beyond the end of a verse or couplet." Well, we all know it. This is a country in which language matters.

I looked for bulges mostly in the warren of streets near the Église St-Sulpice: Mabillon, Lobineau, Canettes, Guisarde, Ciseaux. The rue Mabillon was first called rue de la Foire, offering access as it did to the Foire St-Germain, established in 1486 and eventually a complex of columned buildings and hundreds of vendors and shops. More splendid than any modern-day mall, it featured at its height, not only the finest of goods, but also theaters, tightrope walkers, marionettes, magicians, exhibitors of wild animals, and games of chance. The present Marché St-Germain, in the rectangle formed by the rues Lobineau, Mabillon, Clément, and Félibien, is the Foire's pale and much smaller successor. I was most hopeful in my search for bulges in the rue des Ciseaux, opened in 1429 and only sixteen feet wide. Or in the rue des Canettes, which already existed in the year 1260. I did find, on the façade of No. 18, the sculpted medallion representing four ducks preening and cavorting in a pond. The medallion replaces the earlier sign that in 1636 gave the street its current name.

One could think I was being lunatic about my bulge. The building had, after all, been in place for over three hundred years. It had recently undergone, and was continuing to undergo, significant renovations. I even began to chide myself. I had always been afraid to be simply happy. I had no confidence that the universe was a safe or benevolent place. I was always worried about something. Why look for trouble? Why not just assume that things would work out? It seemed like sound advice. But then I learned something else: *I was not the only one concerned about the building's façade.*

I first met my fellow apartment owners at the *assemblée générale*—the owners' meeting, held a couple of months after

I bought the apartment. I wasn't sure what to expect. When I arrived, the group was already deep in conversation, sitting on medieval-looking campstools in the office of an agency for troubled youth that occupied one of the building's boutiques. I introduced myself. No one said a word, though there was a sort of pause of acknowledgment before they resumed their discussion. I found myself a stool.

It became immediately clear that some of the owners wanted to proceed right away with further repairs to the building; others wanted a *"petit souffle"*—a breather. A woman who looked to be in her sixties, with gray hair coiffed in finger waves reminiscent of the 1920s or '30s, would pay nothing, she said, until her boutique's WC was repaired. An exuberant, preppy young man, who owned the entire fourth floor and much of the fifth—which he planned eventually to turn into a duplex—was among those who wanted a breather. Sitting somewhat apart, a solid, tweed-suited gentleman, who could have been mayor of a small town in Madame Bovary's neighborhood, said virtually nothing. I couldn't figure out what he owned. The one I considered the most French of them all was the young man in jodhpur boots and a finely cut jacket who owned a tiny pied-à-terre between the first and second floors. I was sure he had sped in from the country in his sports car—he arrived only moments before the meeting broke up. The most American of the group, an outdoorsy man in a red-and-black checked flannel shirt—I could see him living in Portland or Seattle—kept muttering "Jesus Christ!" under his breath in English at various exasperating moments in the conversation. Assuming, correctly, that housing construction was not one of my areas of expertise, a long-faced engineer, at the meeting to advise about building repairs, turned frequently to assure me that the problems were no big deal.

I had dressed down for the meeting, thinking that in such a

THE QUALITY OF THE LINE

modest building, the owners might be of modest means. So I wasn't at all prepared for the arrival of the *avocate*—the lawyer, wrapped in mink and sporting a diamond the size of the sun. She arrived late, all a flurry after a dinner I suspected was romantic, to bring us up to date on legal proceedings with the building behind us in the rue des Quatre Vents. Apparently, a drainpipe connected with that building was channeling water into ours. The pipe had supposedly been fixed, but the leaks continued, and we couldn't proceed with repairs to our building until the pipe was fixed properly. Fumbling with her glasses, the *avocate* read us the latest correspondence, the upshot of which was that the owners of the other building simply refused to listen anymore. As discussion resumed, I couldn't help wondering why we didn't just offer to fix the pipe ourselves instead of going through all this legal rigmarole. It was just a pipe. But I kept my thoughts to myself.

It wasn't until a subsequent *assemblée générale* that I heard questions about the building's soundness. The questions were not, I admit, inspired by the bulge. At least the bulge wasn't mentioned at the meeting (though surely it was part of the collective unconscious). What the questions were inspired by was buses. It appears that a number of bus lines (as I write, there are five) had been routed through the rue St-Sulpice, instead of the wider rue de Vaugirard, because the Vaugirard route would lead the buses past the Sénat at the head of the Luxembourg Gardens. The senators feared that too many passing buses might disturb their deliberations.

With so many buses throttling through the street, the question was as apparently dire as anything I might think up: "Is the building moving?" No one at the meeting seemed particularly upset at the prospect. But presumably we needed to know before embarking on the *ravalement*—the restoration of the masonry and stucco of the building's façade. A *témoin,* a

small patch of plaster, would be applied to a fissure on the side wall of the building to measure any detectable displacement. Strangely enough, I felt more reassured than alarmed about the test. It would by definition address the issue of the bulge.

Don't get me wrong. I didn't spend all of my time thinking about the building's potential collapse. I loved my apartment, the sun shining through the slightly rippled glass of the casement windows, the carved stone mantle with the seashell-shaped medallion at its center, the cleanly painted white walls. It was some years before I had it entirely furnished, but that never diminished the apartment's warmth. I loved my neighborhood, the view from my windows, the rows of chimney pots against an always changing sky, the tiny *place* at the junction of the rue St-Sulpice and the rue de Condé, with its red-awninged restaurant and its globe-shaped street lamp. The coffee and tea shop near the corner of the rue St-Sulpice and rue Mabillon offered blends and roasts too numerous to count. I was brought up short on my first visit when the proprietor asked me which blend of coffee I preferred. I didn't know what to say. I knew what I wanted only by what they called it in America: "French roast." On the fountain at the center of the place St-Sulpice, overlooked by the façade of St-Sulpice Church, sculpted lions guard four seated bishops as water pours into the fountain's basin. It is true what Ernest Hemingway wrote in *A Moveable Feast*. Pigeons do perch on the heads of the bishops. I snapped a photograph of one of the bishops, on his throne, with a pigeon standing on his head. The goofiness of the scene was irresistible.

But always, no matter where I was or what I was doing, I was savoring the language, testing it, tasting and feeling the words on my tongue. Those beautiful words. A friend of mine, an organist, said to me recently, "For me, French has always been another form of music." In the Luxembourg Gardens, I happened on a sign that read *"Pelouse autorisée"*—walking on grass permitted. I pronounced the words to myself, *"pelouse autorisée."* Such a beautiful word, *pelouse*. But what does it mean to say that? I wondered. What is it that makes a word beautiful?

I decided to make a list. I'd forget about bulges. This time, I would walk the streets of my neighborhood and write down every beautiful word I saw—on signs, on store fronts, in shop windows. The words were everywhere: *pelouse*—lawn, *vitrine en cours*—window in progress (sometimes I chose phrases), *tabatière*—snuffbox, *église*—church, *amour*—love, *jardin*—garden, *colombier*—dovecote, *gravures anciennes*—antique engravings, *mincir*—to lose weight, *moulin à vent*—windmill, *carrefour*—intersection, *sculpteur*—sculptor, *peinture*—painting, *fontaine*—fountain, *fleurie*—in bloom, *rossignol*—nightingale, *désirs*—desires, to name a few.

French is a language of vowels. As opposed to English, which is a language of consonants. In English, the vowel can virtually disappear and the speaker will be understood. In French, each vowel is a clear, musical sound (with such exceptions as the so-called mute "e"). Even the length of the vowel can signal a different word, as in *patte*—paw, and *pâte*—pastry. In each the "a" sound is the same, but in *patte* it is shorter, in *pâte* comparatively longer. (Context also plays a role in understanding the spoken language, as even the French are not always careful to make such distinctions. Furthermore, there are many homonyms in French. But that's another story.)

There are nineteen vowel sounds in French, officially at least, four of which are nasals: in, un, an, on. Among the consonants are three nasals: m, n, gn. I came to think that, above all, it is the extension of these sounds—the vowels, the nasals, which are intrinsically resonant, combined with the delicacy of the consonants that makes French words beautiful. *Pelouse, tabatière, colombier, anciennes, moulin à vent.* The way the "t" springs softly off the back of the upper teeth, sinking into the "ye" sound of the "i" to launch the extended "air" in *tabatière."* The extended "n" in *anciennes,* finished by the barely sounded final "e." The sequence of vowel sounds in *moulin à vent.* To form them is like mouthing a scale or a chord. So often the extension is brought about by the final "r": *sculpteur, intérieur, coiffeur, douleur.* For me, the word *douleur* epitomizes my sense of French as a language of delicacy and longing.

A word can be beautiful even if its meaning is not. (Not everyone will agree with me on this point.) Two words come immediately to mind: *ordure*—filth, and *viol*—rape. For me, the beauty is in sliding, sinking into the "ure" of *ordure* (I manage to ignore the sum of these parts that would have me sinking into filth), and the "ye" sound again in *viol* lifting the tongue over the open "o" to the extended "l." I have seen the word *ordure* in more than one poem. In *"Les Larmes de Saint Pierre,"* François Malherbe writes of *"Leurs pieds, qui n'ont jamais les ordures pressées"* (Their feet which have never stepped in filth). The word *ordure* contributes mightily to the lyricism of the line. On the other hand, a friend of mine points out that, as a native French-speaker, she could never separate the sound of the word *viol* from its meaning. Perhaps it is because French is not my native tongue that I can hear the sound pure. (*Viol* has a homonym that does combine beauty in sound and meaning—the stringed musical instrument *viole*. But that's beside my point.)

When I speak French, I am more conscious of the changing shape of my mouth, of tongue against teeth and palate, the movements of mouth, tongue, lips in forming the words—a conscious physical act, like playing a musical instrument. I am aware of the more extensive movement of my mouth in pronouncing the vowels, the gentle tongue forming the consonants, the *netteté*—the cleanness and clarity with which French vowels and consonants are spoken. A French friend points to the clear-cut vowel sounds in French, as opposed to English. She refers to the "waves" in English vowel sounds which make learning English difficult. I didn't know what she meant, until I caught myself pronouncing the word *mot* in a lazy English way. It came out something like mow-oo, something that would never happen in French correctly pronounced.

In 1917, the English poet A. E. Housman turned to André Gide and asked, "How is it that every nation has produced poetry except France?" My immediate response on learning of Housman's question was an incredulous: "What?" Nothing could have seemed more incongruous. Here was someone saying that the poetic tradition I feel so akin to is not poetry at all. It struck me as absurd.

Jacques Barzun's *Essay on French Verse for Readers of English Poetry* offers a more learned and more measured response. (An eminent scholar and author, Barzun was a literary advisor at Scribner's when I was there, and a true polymath—a word I don't use lightly. In fact, I'm not sure I've ever used it at all—at least not in describing an acquaintance.) Barzun recapitulates the charges leveled at French poetry: "an endless series of twelve-syllable lines riming feebly;"—Barzun uses the variant spelling of *rhyme*—"a preference for abstractions occasionally rising into a *tirade*, which at best is oratory, not poetry; an invariably moral or social subject matter—not a bird or flower in a thousand lines—all this is but mannered prose etiolated by needlessly arbitrary rules of versification. The heavily Latinized vocabulary lacks immediacy and evocative power, and being sounded without accent yields no rhythm." A pretty powerful indictment. But the word "flower" makes me think immediately of these lines from Ronsard's *"Les Amours de Cassandre"*:

THE QUALITY OF THE LIN

> "Mignonne, allons voir si la rose
> Qui ce matin avait déclose
> Sa robe de pourpre au Soleil,..."

(Darling, let's go see if the rose/Which this morning had opened/Its purple gown to the Sun....) Not a twelve-syllable line, and there it is, a rose (though admittedly used later as a moral lesson). But isn't that an enjambment between the second and third lines? What the indictment really applies to is the French neoclassical tradition, which begins around 1600 with the above-mentioned Malherbe and a few other poets seeking to rein in the supposed extravagances and carelessness of French poetry up to that time. Poets of the neoclassical period still used lines of six, eight, or ten syllables, but the more "noble," twelve-syllable alexandrine predominated. According to Barzun, Malherbe's *juste cadence,* or "due measure," for the alexandrine required the following: "the break (cesura) must come exactly in the middle; that is, each half line must make up a complete unit of meaning; the whole line must also be self-contained—no runover." It is at this time too that "the great purge" was launched to prune the French language, whose vocabulary was cluttered and overblown, to eliminate unnecessary synonyms, and to define clearly the words that remained. The rules of versification tightened. Excluded from the alexandrine were: "all common expressions that contain a hiatus [two vowel sounds pronounced in succession, one at the end of a word, the other at the start of the next]; all words that might cause a rime between the sixth syllable and the later or previous twelfth; all words at the cesura that end in a mute e before a following consonant." It does seem almost unimaginably difficult to write a poem and at the same time to remember all these strictures. But that is where the art is. As Barzun points out, the great poets, like Corneille, accepted the strictures as a whole, but "did as they pleased whenever they wanted." Part of the esthetic pleasure was in the deviation. The reason for the hoots and jeers at the Comédie-Française over the opening lines of *Hernani* was that Hugo's enjambment was particularly egregious. It was also widely known in advance that the play was to be a challenge to the established order.

I began to wonder if I could write some poem lines using my beautiful words. Perhaps even in the neoclassical tradition, before Chénier, Lamartine, and Victor Hugo began the loosening of the rules. I would try to remember caesura, hiatus, masculine and feminine rhymes (feminine—rhymes that end with a mute "e," masculine, those that don't. Their pattern of alternation is another important element of French versification.). I would be conscious of the way in which elision and liaison blend each word into a greater musical line, thus contributing to the poem's forward propulsion, its flow. As a non-native speaker, I might never fully grasp the most subtle nuances that bring the number of vowel sounds to far more than nineteen. Nor might I master what Barzun refers to as "the variable accentuation that is characteristic of the language," the change in the way a word is stressed depending on the meaning and "even more according to the character of the speaker." To top it off, I read in Theodora Bosanquet's *Paul Valéry* that for Valéry the touchstone of poetry was "the correct management of the mute 'e.'" I wasn't sure what all was involved in the correct management of the mute "e," which most often occurs at the end of a word, beyond the fact that in poetry it is sounded before a consonant, to link the word to the one that follows, and mute, that is, elided, before a vowel. My knowledge wasn't profound, but I wanted to try to turn my words into a beautiful musical line. Perhaps the language itself would rescue me.

Well, it did and it didn't. A mute "e" kept appearing where I

THE QUALITY OF THE LINE

didn't want an extra syllable; the proper noun for the sense turned out to be feminine, necessitating, again, an extra syllable for the *"de la"* instead of the masculine *"du."* One attempt, after several that were unsatisfactory, turned out to have only feminine rhymes. And working with so few words, I had very few rhymes at my disposal. A further stumbling block, and this surprised me, was my sense of the natural length of the line. As a native English-speaker, I tended to think in pentameters. Or at least I repeatedly found myself composing five-syllable half-lines. My greatest handicap, of course, was that my base vocabulary was the words I had seen in my neighborhood—fifty-nine words or expressions in all. As most of the words in this base vocabulary were nouns, I was obliged to add other parts of speech when needed. So, here are the lines I came up with:

> *"Rossignol, doux chanteur d'une ancienne aventure,*
> *Au jardin capturé en traits fins de peinture,*
> *Brave oiseau silencieux, rallume ton désir,*
> *Chante-moi, si tu peux, ton lointain souvenir."*

(Nightingale, sweet singer of a long ago adventure/Captured in the garden in delicate strokes of paint/Good silent bird, rekindle your desire/Sing to me, if you can, your distant memory.) It may lack the requisite loftiness and grandeur—it's about a bird, after all. (Along with all the strictures came a taste for elegance and circumlocution, a codification of the language, a sense of *bon usage* that makes the French even today highly sensitive to substandard usage, not to mention outright mistakes.) But still, structurally, it has four alexandrines, caesuras in the right place, two feminine followed by two masculine rhymes, mute "e"s behaving as they should. And it's all reasonably melodic. It was some time before I perceived the hiatus between *capturé* and *en* in the second line. As hiatuses go, it is not a bad one. To my ear the flow of the "é" into the *"en"* is beautiful. And the hiatus does take place at the caesura, which lessens "the pain." I paged through my anthologies of French poetry. When I found two hiatuses at the caesura in Malherbe himself, I felt exonerated.

    It wasn't until even later that I learned the implication of long and short vowels to the French poetic line. In a luncheon talk in the salons of the Sénat, sponsored by DLF (the association *Défense de la langue française)*, scholar and author Vladimir Volkoff spoke of how long and short vowels, as opposed to tonic stresses, combine in French poetry to create the equivalent of poetic feet, thus providing a rhythmical diversity, a music, far more complex than the phrases "endless series of twelve-syllable lines" or "being sounded without accent yields no rhythm" would suggest. Since what stress there is in French tends to fall on the final syllable, it is iambs and anapests that we see most often: iamb, short/long; anapest, short/short/long—though, of course, the stresses are not as strong as those in English. The music of the alexandrine resides in part in the continuing variation of poetic feet within that sequence of twelve-syllable lines. In scanning my own poem lines, I see that all but possibly the final line are made up of anapests. Ideally, there would be more variety. That's something to remember next time.

    Had George been with me, I wonder if I would have become so possessed by the bulge. I know he wasn't impressed with the apartment at first glance. He expected something grander, something more, well, *"style Haussmann."* I think of him standing in the living room, puzzled, not saying a word, trying to bring his idea of a proper Paris apartment—high ceilings, large rooms, beautifully paneled doors, boiseries—into line with the more Bohemian reality I had chosen. It wasn't until our next trip to Paris that everything came into focus. George

THE QUALITY OF THE LINE

stood at the window as I sat on the floor poring through French decorating magazines. We were waiting for France Télécom to come and install the phone. I had asked for two phones, one for the living room and one for the bedroom. When I asked what styles were available, I had one of my first bumps into French monopoly and bureaucracy: "We'll bring you a phone and if you don't like it you can turn it in for another one."

In the end I got only one phone. "The cord is long," the installer told me. "You can carry it from room to room." The phone was beige, with big, black sans serif numerals, and an earphone on a cord at the back so someone else could listen in. It struck me at the time as immensely stylish and, with the extra earpiece, exotic. George and I stood over it, our newly arrived telephone, ensconced there on the carpet. I had ordered some furniture, but there wasn't a stick of it in the apartment at the time. Still, something had changed. As we stood there, I felt a surge of well-being and knew that George felt it too. He looked down at the phone with a trace of a smile, his hands in his pockets. The presence of the phone legitimized us in some way. It meant that we belonged.

George died approximately three months to the day after I bought the apartment. He woke up one morning in New York, suffering from chest pain and shortness of breath. Neither of us recognized the gravity of what was happening, or at least I didn't, as he lay on the bed waiting for the incident to pass. He had suffered from angina for years. But the pain persisted. I called our doctor, who told us to get to the emergency room right away. George didn't want to go. I gathered his clothes and helped him to dress. I remember him at the hospital, propped against pillows, in a white shirt and navy trousers. He refused to complain. They gave him some morphine, but it just made him throw up. He was having a heart attack. He would live for two and a half more days.

Sometimes I wonder that I even survived George's dying. For months afterward, the pain of it weighed like a stone around my heart. I sobbed at the least provocation. I slept fitfully, plagued by nightmares. Now, when I think of him, I think first of his delight. George had taught me how to live. He had taught me to seize opportunities, to remember what is important, to view human foibles with humor and generosity. I couldn't imagine the bond between us being broken. We completed each other. I idolized and adored him. The touch of his long, slender fingers was magic. And now he was gone.

Only weeks after George died, I got a call from Paris at five o'clock in the morning. There had been a leak, a not unusual event in the city's older buildings, and the ceiling of my apartment had been severely damaged. (Actually, what they told me was that my ceiling had fallen in, but that proved not to be the case.) Still dizzy with grief, I returned to Paris. I spoke with the engineer, the one I had met at the *assemblée générale,* and the contractor, who had handled the apartment renovations, about the repairs. Then, notified that the beds I had ordered on our previous trip were ready to be delivered, I waited, just as George and I had waited for the phone. I had decided on two narrow French twin beds in white bamboo, fearing that a double bed would overwhelm the room. But when the deliveryman arrived, there was only one bed. I couldn't help wondering: Did the universe know when I placed the order that George was going to die?

When I am in Paris, I like to walk along the rue de l'Ancienne-Comédie through the carrefour de Buci, and up the rue Mazarine to the Pont des Arts and the Institut de France. It has become an oft-repeated pilgrimage. On the Pont des Arts, looking downriver in the golden haze of sunset, I know I am in the most beautiful place in the world. Cradled between the long reach of the Louvre to my right, the Institut and the line of trees

to the Musée d'Orsay to my left, the river flows in the hush of evening toward the elongated arches of the Pont du Carrousel. Beyond, I can see the rounded glass roof of the Grand Palais. At the far end of the Louvre, the Pavillon de Flore, silhouetted against the sky, becomes the enchanted house of a fairy tale.

I still feel George standing there, framed by the Institut across the street, asking me, "Would you like to have an apartment here someday?" I look again at that beautiful building. I feel the pull of its beckoning arms, the rich diversity of its decorative elements—extended balustrades, garlanded urns in the roof topped with Statue of Liberty-like flames, lunettes like gilded dormers in the dome. At night, spotlights and thin lines of lights along the cornices cast a gentle gold light intermingled with shadow. The lights are angled to leave shadows, so that the whole becomes a chiaroscuro of mystery, possibility, and wonder. The building is passion contained in reason. There is a linearity about even the most decorative architecture here that lightens and, at the same time, grounds it. It is the line that one sees in French poetry, in which elision and liaison, the absence of strong accent, the mute "e" that lengthens the accentuated vowel preceding it, while at the same time injecting tonality or emotion (I read this last in *The New Oxford Companion to Literature in French),* all contribute to the clarity of the line. The prominence of line over volume, the shape and unity of the line, are the touchstones of Paris's beauty.

What is the French word for "bulge"? Would my bulge have seemed less malign in French? Would some beautiful French equivalent make it seem gentler and less threatening? I look in my dictionary. The French word for bulge is *bombement*. I'm not sure this is better, with its subliminal reference to both the French and English words for "bomb." On the other hand, I had ordered chairs with seats that were *"bombés."* The word *bombement* derives from *"bomber,"* to swell.

It's been years now since I've looked at the bulge. I even wonder, if I looked for it now, whether I would see anything that I would call a bulge. The results of the test with the *"témoin"* were *"négatif."* Perhaps that reassured me, allowed me to let any question of bulges drift out of my mind over time. Or perhaps, unconsciously, I took on a longer view of history, an acceptance of the imperfections that arise over the life of a building centuries old. It was just as well. I had a conversation recently with an Englishwoman who had lived in France for over twenty years. When I told her about the bulge and the reassurance I derived from the thought that the owners wouldn't have replumbed and rewired a building that wasn't sound, she replied, "That's English reasoning, not French." An English person, she told me, on seeing a property he liked, would have it inspected before buying. In fact, the bank providing the mortgage would require it. The same holds true for Americans. A French person would simply buy the property. French banks don't require an inspection. So if a French person isn't worried about a building's soundness on buying, why would he worry when replumbing and rewiring? My attempt to reassure myself had no basis in practice. It's a good thing I didn't know that at the time.

RES MEDICAE

Y‌EARS BEFORE I BOUGHT THE PARIS APARTMENT, when I first knew George, I was always afraid that he might die. Not that there was anything particularly frail about him. On the contrary. His stance was stalwart in his London-tailored suits, or in his riding clothes—he still "rode to hounds." He was equally likely to be found slithering under one of his antique cars to adjust some nut or valve. The light in his eyes alone should have reassured me. But there was no denying his numerical age. His thick sweep of hair was the color of moonlight. From early childhood, I had been taught not to care too much, not to luxuriate in good fortune—God didn't like that. I couldn't believe that this man who had become the center of my life, whose mere presence made my heart soar, would not be taken from me.

There had even been some legitimate scares. The prostate surgery, for example, which had involved a significant hemorrhage. (He had also suffered a mild heart attack, but that was before I knew him.) The worst of these scares was his bout with septicemia, which left him in a coma, with the doctors themselves fearing for his life. By some miracle, or some act of will, he began to improve. It took months for him to regain his equilibrium. We would be walking together down some New York street and all of a sudden he would be gone, wheeling behind me to grab onto a lamppost or street sign to keep from falling. But again he recovered. Once we were married, and with the passage of time, his resilience must have made its way into my subconscious. He became so much a part of me that I stopped fearing his not being there. It just didn't occur to me anymore. So I scarcely knew what to do with the sight of him, lying limp in a Paris hospital, uncomprehending, his voice a mere exhalation of breath.

It was only recently that I had bought the tiny apartment in the rue St-Sulpice. A pied-à-terre, really, it represented more to me than an occasional getaway, though that might have been reason enough to buy it. The apartment was, above all, an extension of my love for the French language, a physical place that would make the language real. I imagined it as an embodiment of the language, and of the culture the language reflects and articulates. As such it was a repository of incalculable treasure—not to mention entertainment.

We had traveled again to Paris in early December to look for furniture and to take care of such mundane tasks as getting the electricity turned on. Shortly after buying the apartment, I had engaged the services of Madame M, a lovely French woman who gave French lessons to transplanted Americans and looked out for their apartments when they were away. Under her auspices, the *serrure à cinq points,* the five-point lock, required by my French homeowner's policy, had already been installed on the front door. I had to laugh when I saw it. I had been told that while mugging was the crime of choice in New York, in Paris thieves were more likely to break into apartments to steal the silver. Interlocking steel bars an inch and a half wide, secured to the interior side of the door, locked into the door frame at four points, top, bottom, and two on one side. A shorter bar, representing the fifth point, reinforced the door latch. I could hardly believe my eyes. Such a clumsy, over-the-top contraption. It was worthy of a maximum security prison. No French refinement there.

I found the local office of Électricité de France, more commonly known as EDF, behind a bleak, minimalist storefront in the rue de Rennes. I could have asked Madame M to deal with the electric company, but I regarded such responsibilities as part of the challenge of entering into French life and I wanted to experience going there myself. (I had asked Madame M to have the lock installed because the insurance company insisted I have it done right away.) Armed only with my street address and the fact that my apartment location was *troisième étage, droite*—third floor, on the right as you reach the landing—I soon discovered how inadequate I was to the task. Before turning on my electricity, the man behind the counter told me, they had to know the volume of my *cumulus* and the *marque* and *puissance* of my *convecteurs*. What? After thinking a moment, I figured that the *convecteurs* were my wall-mounted electric heaters. But I certainly didn't know what *marque,* or brand, they were, or their *puissance*—wattage. The *cumulus,* he subsequently explained, was my *chauffe-eau,* or hot-water heater. But I'd never seen it. It was hidden above my bathroom ceiling. They had to show me color photos of various types of appliance so that I could point to the *convecteurs* most closely resembling my own. Then they sent me home to call the contractor who had handled the apartment renovations to find out what the volume of my *cumulus* was. As it turns out, the volume was 150 liters. The reason they had to know all this was that in France one's electrical service is based on the total *puissance* the dwelling requires.

RES MEDICAE

The day that landed George in the hospital began innocently enough. Since our arrival, I had been carrying around pages ripped from French decorating magazines—*Maison et Jardin, Maison Française*—picturing items of furniture I particularly liked. I had decided not to follow the flea market route, which seemed a haphazard way to furnish an apartment from scratch. It also required time and expertise. And if thieves were going to break into the apartment when I wasn't there, I didn't want to lose anything expensive or irreplaceable. Most of my choices were traditional French styles, Empire, Louis XV. But one modern piece had caught my eye in leafing through a magazine, an Artelano desk, slender-legged, *"en érable teinté et laque noire"*—in tinted maple and black lacquer. I had hoped to spot it in some store window as George and I strolled the Paris streets, and eventually even ordered one in a small Paris shop on the basis of the magazine write-up. But somehow I didn't feel we'd gotten the job done. I can still hear George saying, "Let's cut to the chase." He ordered a car and driver and off we went to Art de Vivre à Orgeval, 36 kilometers west of Paris. The magazine billed Art de Vivre as *"le plus grand showroom de la maison."* There, in a looming warehouse space, we found the desk, no longer a picture but the real thing. When we returned to Paris, I went immediately to the shop where I had placed the order to tell them I had found the desk on my own. I couldn't help noting how surprised the staff seemed that I had bothered to come back to let them know.

We went to bed early that night. George had begun to feel ill. I had heard him vomiting in the bathroom. Since there was no furniture in the apartment, we were staying at the small hotel next door. It was one of those hotels in which everything is diminutive. A double bed, small table and chair, and mini-bar left little space for maneuvering, but the ceiling's exposed beams and the bursts of roses on its fabric-covered walls gave the room a compensating charm. And, best of all, the toilet facilities, with their miniature, boxed Roger & Gallet soaps, were attractive and entirely up to date. The presence of the hotel had actually been part of my thinking in buying the apartment; it could serve as relatively inexpensive guest accommodations, should friends or family come to visit.

At 3:30 a.m. I awoke to find George slumped on the edge of the bed, his feet on the floor. I asked him, "Are you okay?"

"Yeah."

He didn't sound convincing. I propped myself up on one elbow.

"What's wrong?" I asked.

"Stomach," he replied.

"Do you want me to bring you a wastebasket?"

"No."

"Are you sure?"

"Yeah."

He put his hands on his knees, holding himself steady. I lay down again, unsure, waiting for him to tell me he was all right. The pale light of the street lamp below shone through the window, highlighting the curve of his back. I reached toward him over the rumpled bedclothes, resting my hand at his side, but not touching him. I didn't want to intrude on his unease. He rose up slightly, drawing in his breath. Then, in a violent trajectory, he threw up again. I jumped to my feet and, after turning on the light, circled around to his side of the bed. It was then that I realized he was throwing up blood.

I'd like to be able to say that I knew right away what to do. George sat on the edge of the bed, stunned, as I moved to clean up. But it was futile. The blood had seeped into the carpet, splattered into the fabric on the walls. It was nearly four in the morning, a Sunday. Could I wait until daylight to try to find a doctor? How serious was this? Should I call an ambulance? I had the phone number of a friend's French stepbrother, Pierre, who lived in Paris and happened to be a doctor. Did I dare call him at this hour? It occurred to me that it was only 10 p.m. in New York. I called our doctor's office there and spoke to his service. Within minutes he called me back. The situation did warrant waking Pierre, he said. And I should call an ambulance.

I dialed Pierre's number. He could tell me which hospital to go to. A woman answered. When I asked to speak to Pierre, she told me this wasn't his number anymore. I apologized profusely. She was extremely civil, unhurried. I was more than impressed at her kindness in being awakened at four o'clock in the morning. Especially since this was a city not known for its patience with blundering Americans.

There was nothing left but to try to get an ambulance. I asked Hotel Reception to make the call. Soon enough I received a return call from SAMU—*Service d'Aide Médicale Urgente*—asking for a full account of the situation. How much blood did he throw up? When? What color was it? After a thorough grilling, they agreed to send an ambulance. I got dressed. George lay on the bed, his arm draped across his forehead. I had managed to get him into a shirt and trousers. I felt so closed in by the night dark, the utter silence of the street. Forty minutes went by. I grew more and more agitated, fidgeting with the contents of my purse, tidying the room, watching George's closed eyes. What could be taking so long? I called Reception again. Finally, at 5:30 a.m., the phone rang. The ambulance—*Assistance Publique*—had arrived.

The two attendants entered our fifth-floor room, filling it with their authority. They asked me to get George into his coat and shoes. Then they hoisted him up, holding one of his arms over each shoulder, their free hands lifting his legs into a sitting position. George managed a small, embarrassed smile. I grabbed my own coat—it was unusually cold in Paris—and followed them into the hallway. Step by step, they carried him down the successive flights of the narrow, winding staircase—the elevator was too small for such a maneuver—through the hotel lobby, and outside, into the back of their shiny new Citroën ambulance. I asked where we were going. To Hôpital Cochin, they said. I knew nothing of Paris hospitals. *C'est un bon hôpital?* I asked. Oh yes, they assured me. But I had no way of knowing.

    Eventually I would discover how large a complex the hospital was. But as we arrived, in the dark, I saw only the large lighted sign, "URGENCES," and the barren, empty waiting room, all beige. I remember the room as being full of benches of the same color, but that may be a trick of memory. It seemed ominous to me that the emergency room staff was asleep. This was nothing like the emergency rooms on American television. But soon enough a young intern and a nurse appeared, seemingly competent and adroit. George was wheeled into a complex of rooms behind a partition. Forbidden to accompany him, I sat alone on one of the benches. The young doctor, who spoke no English, darted back and forth between the examining room and the waiting room, seeking details of George's medical history. Once he had retreated, I remained the only person in the large, anonymous room. There was little comfort in the room's drabness--all that beige, not a hint of color, no embellishment to suggest a human touch. I heard the quiet rustle of activity as they worked on George. I took off my coat, resettled myself on the bench. Minutes passed. All of a sudden, I heard thumps, the sound of thrashing, urgent voices. What were they doing to him? I forced myself to stay where I was. The young doctor reappeared again. He had the wiry quickness of so many Parisians.

    "*Comment dit-on 'avalez' en anglais?*" he asked. How do you say "*avalez*" in English?

RES MEDICAE

"Swallow," I replied. My ability to translate distracted me for a moment from my feelings of helplessness. I felt momentarily accomplished, more important than I really was.

He rushed back behind the partition. I heard him urging George repeatedly to "swallow," but I doubted that in his condition George would understand the doctor's nearly unrecognizable rendering of the word. When I was finally allowed in, they were pulling an endoscopy tube out of his throat. They had been examining his esophagus and his stomach. George's head jerked to one side, then the other. He seemed nearly delirious. The sight of him left me almost frantic.

I had to go to the admissions office before George could be moved. An orderly I hadn't seen before led me out of the building into the pre-dawn light, where we crossed to a large, Victorian-looking, blond brick building that housed *Renseignements/Accueil*—Information/Reception. It was all I could do to hold myself together in the eerie semi-dark, to project an air of assurance, to keep out of my voice the trembling I felt inside. I didn't want the orderly to fear he might be stuck with some wailing relative. I knew that these arrangements were part of my job, and I wanted George to be able to depend on me. George admired strength and dignity. I answered the questions at admissions as calmly as I could. After all the necessary forms were filled out, I was asked to make a deposit of 23,600 francs, which would cover ten days of hospitalization. That represented a daily charge of 2,360 francs, or, depending on the exchange rate, around four hundred dollars a day. I had to accept the fact that George's Medicare would not pay for a hospital stay in France. Still, 23,600 francs seemed like a huge amount to pay up front. What if he wasn't going to be there for ten days? In the end, I was allowed to pay by the day. And each day, before visiting hours, I would present myself at the cashier's window to hand over a check, written on my Paris bank account.

George was swathed in blankets on my return to the emergency room, on a gurney with a plastic roof to protect against rain. His destination was *Réanimation*—Intensive Care. *Réanimation,* such a wonderful and fearful word: to make alive again, to revive, from *anima,* meaning "breath," "soul." On his arrival in the ICU, the nurses settled him into bed, naked, but still he couldn't stop thrashing. It was eight o'clock in the morning. "You'll have to leave the room now," one of the nurses told me. It was time for the patients' *toilettes.* "We'll call you," she said, "when the anesthesiologist arrives."

What could she mean, "anesthesiologist"?

"Are they going to operate on him?" I asked.

"No, no," she reassured me. "They're not going to operate on him. But he's the type of doctor to examine this problem."

I still didn't understand how an anesthesiologist fit into the picture, but as long as they weren't going to anesthetize him, I decided to let it be. I told George I'd be right outside, but I wasn't sure he heard me. I didn't want to leave the room. As I reached the doorway, I turned to see George trying to get his leg over the bedrail. The nurse eased him back into a lying position. I stood motionless, dismayed. The nurse looked toward me. I backed into the hallway to find a seating area where I could wait.

Two hours later I was still waiting. Fed up, I started back to George, only to find the doctor already there.

"We're going to do a bronchoscopy in late morning," he said. "But you'll have to leave now."

They had George in restraints to contain his thrashing.

On the way back to the hotel, I sat in the back seat of the taxi, holding George's *"affaires"* in my lap. The nurses had wrapped his clothes, his coat, and his shoes in plastic, and had tied the package with string. Even then, as the taxi made its way through the quiet morning streets, I recognized how pitiable I looked. It was as though George had died and I had been sent home with his effects.

The sight of him lying in the hospital bed, his body twisting against the restraints, his face frantic, left me feeling bludgeoned, the part of me that would have cried out or burst into sobs stunned into silence. I was running on nerves. It was all I could do to go through the motions. Even in the December cold, the Luxembourg Gardens became a temporary refuge. On my return to the hotel, I had managed to get Pierre's current phone number and had found him at home. By some miracle of serendipity, l'Hôpital Cochin was his hospital; he would arrange for one of his residents to do the bronchoscopy. George would be in good hands. With that reassurance, I called George's younger son, Jack, a California pediatrician, to fill him in.

In the Luxembourg Gardens, waiting for the hospital's visiting hours to begin, I sat in a metal armchair at the foot of the *bassin,* looking over the fountain to the Palais de Luxembourg, with its *tricolore*—the blue, white, and red French flag—rippling against the sky. I began to understand the calming power of symmetry, the way the *palais* anchors and presides over the long extent of park, the arcing balustrades echoing the lines of the *bassin,* the parallel rectangles of flower beds set within larger rectangles of lawn. In summer, urns on the balustrades would spill over with flowers. I saw how the symmetries of the *palais* itself reinforce the feeling of serenity, the strong horizontals of the exterior rustication, the vertical rhythms of the pilasters, the arched windows at ground level, all held in exquisite equipoise. I have read that a guiding ideal in French garden design is an order that corrects nature and at the same time polices human passion. However ambiguous that ideal might be, I felt the calm the garden engenders. *Ordre et beauté*—to recall Baudelaire's immortal words.

At 1:00 p.m. I was back at the hospital. George lay in a private room, the rails of his bed raised, less agitated now, but still disoriented. He was no longer restrained. One of the nurses gave me a sterile robe to put on over my clothes so that I could sit with him. The endoscopy had revealed ulcerations of the esophagus and stomach, with blood clots in the stomach. A lung x-ray had shown pneumonia of the right inferior lobe and an enlarged heart. Blood cultures indicated the pneumonia would be sensitive to Erythromycin. (In the end, they had not done a bronchoscopy.) On his arrival in the ICU, his temperature was 39 degrees centigrade, 102.2 degrees Fahrenheit. Though his mind remained in a world of its own and there was little I could do to help, it was a relief for me just to be near him. I wanted somehow to take care of him, to protect him. But the hospital's limited visiting hours wouldn't allow me much time even to be there. I asked one of the residents to arrange for a private nurse to stay with George overnight. That way, someone would be at hand if he needed anything, or if he tried again to scale the rails of the bed.

"Ce n'est pas évident," he replied.

"Qu'est-ce que ça veut dire, 'évident'?" I asked. I didn't know what he meant by *"évident,"* which means what you would think it meant in English—evident.

"Ce n'est pas simple," he said. That's not so easy.

He would do his best, he said. But apparently, private nurses were not commonplace in Paris hospitals. When the nurse arrived during evening visiting hours, she seemed willing enough. I explained that, basically, I just wanted her to keep George safe, but I think she found that a puzzling assignment.

I had plotted my route from the hotel to the hospital using my *Métro* map (I had just bought an apartment, but still didn't know Paris well). And so, twice each day—visiting hours were from 1:00 to 1:30, and 6:30 to 7:30—I would board the *Métro* at the Odéon station in the boulevard St-Germain and travel to Châtelet-les-Halles. There I would change to the RER *(Réseau Express Régional),* which would take me to Port-Royal, the station closest to the hospital. It was a fairly unpleasant trip. Châtelet-les-Halles is a voluminous underground station, with dull, wide platforms and passageways flooded with people. Often enough, some young man would come thundering up behind me to jump over the turnstile, or push his way through on someone else's ticket. It wasn't until years later that I discovered I could have boarded the RER at Saint-Michel, only one stop from Odéon. Furthermore, the hospital was only blocks from the southern edge of the Luxembourg Gardens. In my distraction, I had envisioned it way off to some murky, distant southeast. How different the journey would have been if I'd known that I could walk there.

And so, twice each day, I would climb the steps out of the Port-Royal station and turn left on the wide, tree-lined boulevard de Port-Royal, then right on the rue du Faubourg-St-Jacques to No. 27 and the blond brick building that served as the hospital's port of entry. There was an unintentional hint of whimsy in the otherwise sober building, with its multitude of chimneys, the dormers in its sloping slate roof, the flattened arches in a rustier tan over the windows. Behind it stretched the huge complex of buildings, old and new, that made up what was clearly a preeminent medical center. Pierre came every day, a hearty, careful doctor I had met only once before. He was a teenager, I think, with a flop of dark hair falling onto his forehead, when we met as usher and bridesmaid in the wedding of his stepsister, a school friend of mine. As an adult, he looked taller and had filled out, but he retained the boyish charm I remembered. He spoke English fluently, apart from falling victim occasionally to some *faux ami,* or false friend.

(*Faux amis* are French and English words that are apparently equivalent, but which have different meanings.) The one he used most often was "actually," to mean "now." He was thinking of the French *"actuellement,"* which does mean "now."

On the third day of George's hospitalization, I arrived to find he had been moved from *Réanimation* to Salle Cochin, Pavillon Pasteur, which signaled an improvement in his condition, difficult as that was for me to perceive. Dressed now in a hospital gown, he was asleep under a white sheet and blanket, in a private room that reminded me of the sun porch of my grandfather's house when I was a child. Two of the room's walls were made of paneled wood, painted white, with rows of louvered windows to let in air and light—or so I remember them. We could have been in Thomas Mann's *The Magic Mountain*. George stirred groggily and opened his eyes. His eyes were vacant, confused, his cheeks drawn. "Am I in a summer resort?" he asked. I explained that he was in a hospital. In Paris. He closed his eyes and sank back into sleep.

Although George had presented with symptoms of bleeding ulcers and pneumonia, the doctors seemed fixed on his heart. The entries in the small pocket notebook I had bought for Paris addresses and phone numbers gave way after eight or nine pages to notes on George's condition and details of his medical history unknown to me before I was called upon to answer the questions of his Paris doctors. Repeatedly I would return to the hotel to call one New York doctor or another to get the information they needed. On a two-page spread in my notebook were heart-related scribbles: blood loss, low blood pressure, ST depressions on EKG on lateral precordium, increase in cardiac enzymes, non-Q wave infarction, mild left ventricle failure, fluid overload in CCU, July '86—heart failure. How could I not have known this? It was in July '86 that he had the prostate operation. At the time, we had been married for six years. Was I never told? Or did the doctors sugarcoat the information so ably that I didn't grasp what they were saying? Still, what frightened me now, even more than the possibility of renewed heart problems, was the immediate lethargy and weakness he had sunk into, the passiveness. He tried once to stand. I had to wrap my arms around him to hold him up.

Each trip to the hospital found me more anxious. No matter what the illness, I had never seen George virtually robbed of his life force. I could no longer sense the will, the hunger for living that had always been so evident in him. I would reach across to hold his hand, those beautiful, long-fingered hands, or rest my cheek against the edge of the bed, but felt only his profound exhaustion. It seemed he had no reserves to draw on to pull himself back to the world I lived in. I could touch his hand, but I could not entirely reach him.

My experience of the hospital was awash with words. Unfamiliar words, but words easily understood once I realized that medical words in both English and French have the same Greek or Latin roots, and more often than not are equivalent. *Hémorragie,* hemorrhage, *gastrique,* gastric, *oesophage,* esophagus, *fibrillation,* fibrillation, *cardiologue,* cardiologist, *pulmonaire,* pulmonary, *bronchoscopie,* bronchoscopy, *anticoagulant,* anticoagulant. I was becoming used to asking questions. I had been told that, in France, if you don't ask questions, the doctors will assume you don't want to know. The similarity of the words relieved some of my anxiety. If the language was the same, if French and American doctors thought in the same terms, wouldn't that mean that George would get more or less the same medical treatment in Paris as he would get in New York?

In hindsight, it is hard to believe, but when I wasn't visiting George, or calling New York for more details of his medical history, I was looking at furniture for the apartment. It was something to do to fill the time, and a blessed distraction. Even in the direst of circumstances, I think your mind just makes you rest. Amid the medical data transcribed in my notebook were such notations as *"tapis brosse, 35 x 70,"* door mat, 35 by 70 centimeters; "table—68cm with *volets,* drop leaves, down"; "Daisy Simon—*armoire en merisier massif,"* armoire in solid cherry. Daisy Simon stores in the rue d'Assas and boulevard Henri IV sold reproduction antiques. I had drawn myself a floor plan of the apartment, down to the location of *convecteurs* and light sockets, a reflection of the apartment in its fullness: to the left, off the small entrance area, the bedroom with its white walls and its casement window overlooking the street, to the right the bathroom tiled in terra-cotta and white; straight ahead the living room, white-walled too, and with its own casement window and its graceful carved stone fireplace. In the living room, to the right, beyond the door to the kitchen, an alcove extended the length of the far wall.

I had measured each wall, and each segment of wall, in meters and centimeters. Because the façade of the building was not straight, the living room was wider on the fireplace wall (4m 37cm, or 14 plus feet) than on the near wall (4m even, closer to 13 feet). I imagined that such irregularities were not unusual in buildings as old as mine. The bedroom, a closer to pure rectangle, measured 3m 21cm, or 10½ feet, by 2m 77cm, around 9 feet, not counting the recessed casement window which added 27cm, or 10½ inches. The window's depth reflected the thickness of the outside walls.

Sitting on the floor of the living room, brochures and magazine pages spread out in front of me, I would imagine the furniture I had ordered or was considering, each piece in its place: the Artelano desk in the living room alcove, my workspace; the trim, two-cushioned couch facing the fireplace; the drop-leaf dining table from Daisy Simon against the wall next to the window. At the Daisy Simon shop I had sat in every dining chair available, until deciding on chairs in a Directoire style that were also by far the most comfortable. On an earlier visit, admiring a Louis XV-style Provençal armoire, I had wondered how I could even get it into my apartment. Often enough in Paris, large pieces of furniture must be hoisted into apartments through the windows. But no, apparently, the armoire was manufactured in panels that would be assembled by the delivery person once he was inside.

    Throughout, George remained listless, flat on his back in his hospital bed. It was only after three or four days that he began to grasp what was going on around him, or at least what was going on within his field of vision. I would describe my visit to this or that furniture store, or transmit messages from his two sons who remained in the States, and he would respond, though the expression on his face suggested that he wasn't particularly interested. With the doctors and nurses he was obedient and grateful—too grateful. There was none of the usual rapscallion in him. Moved again, this time into Pierre's service in Pavillon Achard, at Pierre's request, he lay resigned for over an hour under my down coat in the chilly hospital room. I asked repeatedly for a blanket, but I got the sense that he didn't think his life warranted the effort to find one.

    Pierre never seemed hurried, and lingered willingly to answer my questions, as well as questions from George's son Jack, who was using me as a conduit between the Paris doctors and the specialists at his California hospital. Repeatedly, the subject came back to George's heart. Although he shared the typical American's mistrust of any medical establishment other than his own, Jack was clearly satisfied that George was in good hands. What we never addressed explicitly was the ultimate prognosis. That was one question I think I was subconsciously afraid to hear the answer to.

In the exchange of information between Paris and California, because I was often translating, I became increasingly aware of the differences between French and English. I was especially attentive to the differences between French and English word order. One example is the simple inversion of subject and verb in a subordinate clause, as in, say, *"Voici les renseignements que m'ont donnés les médecins new-yorkais."* In English one would say "Here is the information that the New York doctors gave me." But in French the subject and verb in the subordinate clause are often inverted, resulting word for word in "that gave me the New York doctors." I remember one day at the hotel, when, in a conversation with the maid, I remarked, *"Oui, c'est ce que dit mon mari,"* yes, that's what my husband says. Her response was, *"Oh, comme vous parlez bien le français!",* suggesting that neglecting the inversion is a mistake—or better, a solecism—heard frequently from native English-speakers. I'm sure it's one I've been guilty of any number of times myself.

The same sort of effect comes with the placement, especially of adjectival or adverbial phrases, before the direct object. In a French hospital one might hear someone say, *"Il a autour de lui une famille très dévouée,"* he has a very devoted family around him. In this instance, unlike in English usage, *"autour de lui,"* around him, comes before not after the "devoted family." In both the inversion above and the placement of these modifying phrases, the strongest word—in rhythm and in meaning—comes at the end of the sentence. (If the most important word appears in the modifying phrase, then the phrase is likely to come at the end.) I remember talking more recently with a friend of mine when I was tired and barely able to summon my French. The telling thing was that if I managed to enunciate the final word in my sentences, she could understand me, even when I more or less mumbled the rest. The comparative lack of tonic stress in French is compensated for in part by a slight stress on the final syllable of a word group, sentence, or poetic line. Placing the important words at the end keeps the sentence from trailing off. Weighted at beginning and end, the sentence is held in equilibrium—again both in cadence and in meaning.

On the fifth day of George's hospitalization, I followed the usual routine—boarded the Métro at the Odéon station, then trekked the long, subterranean passageways of Châtelet-les-Halles to the RER train and Port-Royal. I was no less anxious. Granted, George was no longer delirious, no longer thrashing and banging against the bedrails, or worse, trying to wrench himself free of restraints. But was the profound languor he lay in an improvement? Wasn't that languor even closer to death than the delirium? At least the thrashing and banging showed a will to fight.

I stopped at the cashier's window to drop off another check, then, once paid up for another day, made my way through the complex of hospital buildings to Pavillon Achard. I was so afraid of what I might find. George had simply been like this for too long. I started down the corridor toward his room as the business of the hospital bustled around me. How long could his ebbing strength hold out? I approached his door, steeling myself. I paused. Did I hear voices? George's voice? I turned into his room. And there he was, in a bathrobe, sitting at a table, wolfing down steak, *pommes frites,* salad, rolls, camembert—and making jokes. I could hardly believe my eyes. George speaking English, the *filles de salle,* hospital assistants, giggling, replying in French. I had no idea how much either understood of the other. It didn't really matter. I walked closer, gathered into their welcome. What they were communicating to one another was their delight.

So there I was, all of a sudden, helping George with his menu choices. He was like Lazarus, risen after four days. The joy of it burbled in my throat. Two young women had arrived with notepads and pens. *"Il aime quel genre de nourriture?"* one of them asked me. What kind of food does he like? *"N'importe quoi,"* I replied, he likes everything. (A French friend tells me it would have been better to say *"Il mange de tout"*). But this clearly wasn't specific enough. And so there followed a three-way, bilingual consideration of *viandes, soupes, légumes,* etc., with me in the middle as interpreter. I was touched by their apparent eagerness to please him. Or perhaps they just didn't know what to make of him, this American who no doubt ate goodness knows what. He was already gaining a certain renown around the hospital, referred to by much of the staff as *"celui qui parle anglais,"* the one who speaks English.

The sight of him, sitting in bed now against crisp, white linens, the light of his smile—I could hardly absorb it. I was happy just to sit there, holding his hand, drinking him in with my eyes. He was again my wry prince. Not that the doctors were through with him. Hospital stays in Paris were much longer than those in the States, where he would probably have been wheeled out the following day. In the end he would be there for four more days, undergoing tests, recovering his strength, and even then we had to negotiate his release.

Looking back, I can still sense the underlying gravity in the doctors' assessment of George's condition, the recognition of a peril that remained unspoken and that my mind subconsciously deflected. His temperature had "normalized" by the time I found him eating the steak. A lung x-ray after five days of antibiotics showed the pneumonia improved, though still not entirely resolved, and the same enlargement of the heart. Two echocardiograms, in search of a possible aneurysm of the left ventricle, showed a mitral insufficiency, among other anomalies, but no aneurysm. What remained to be determined, the doctors said, was any previous history of auricular, or atrial, fibrillation (the French use the term *fibrillation auriculaire),* which could be associated with the mitral insufficiency. But I could unearth no mention of fibrillation in the calls to New York.

Still, the mood around George was one of humor and hope. And although he was beginning to get bored, George maintained his essential good spirits, which reassured me. When I was away from the hospital, the city of Paris, my neighborhood itself, offered its own moments not only of comfort but of exaltation: the Luxembourg Gardens, the new apartment, the bells of St-Sulpice. St-Sulpice, the misfit stepchild of Paris churches, built in stages over centuries, even now unfinished, often mocked for its polyglot classical style. On a Sunday morning, a week to the day after George entered the hospital, I sat on the floor of the apartment, my back against the white wall, listening to the bells. Mellifluous. Luminous. Building gradually in intensity. I could close my eyes and see the aura emanating from each rich, resonant tone. I didn't know until later that the bells had names: Caroline, Louise, Marie. (It has been a custom in the Roman Catholic Church to baptize church bells in ceremonies that even include a godmother and a godfather.) Nor did I know the tenuousness of the church's future, the damp that is killing it within. The piecemeal efforts to save it. The bells slowed, grew more quiet. Softer. Dimmer. Until the ultimate silence. I was suspended in the silence. The whole had taken about ten minutes. George always said "My heart is the one thing I can count on. It always comes through on its own."

The price of George's release was another endoscopy. The doctors didn't want him to leave with questions about his condition still unanswered. But George had had enough. And we had plane reservations to New York in a few days. Pierre came to his bedside with a compromise. They would release him, but wanted him first to undergo another endoscopy to be sure the ulcers had healed, and a bronchoscopy to determine

whether the pneumonia had a local cause. "Just imagine what might happen," Pierre warned, "if the ulcers start bleeding again in mid-flight." But he could conjure no such dire eventuality in support of the bronchoscopy. George met him halfway. He would have the endoscopy, but any bronchoscopy could await another day.

Allowed to accompany him to the testing area, I listened from a bench outside the procedure room as George was prepped for the doctor. Again and again, the attendants asked him to turn onto his left side; again and again, he giggled in reply. I poked my head in the door to tell them he didn't speak French very well. "Fine," they said, "then you can stay here and translate." My first impulse was to run. An endoscopy wasn't a procedure I was particularly eager to watch. While I stood waffling in the doorway, the doctor—the Chief of Service this time—swept me with him into the room. I had no choice. I stood behind George as he lay on his side, placed my hand on his hip. *"Ouvrez grand,"* open wide, they urged, as the doctor slid the big, black tube into his mouth. I translated, but I doubt it was necessary. George coughed, coughed again. I felt his body go rigid. But the tube slipped down easily. When the test was completed, the doctor turned to tell me the ulcers were cured. I complimented him on his dexterity, the ease with which the test had gone. He smiled slightly, then swept out of the room without speaking, a master of his domain.

George left the hospital on his feet, not in a wheelchair, as is the custom in American hospitals. I had arrived earlier that morning with a complete set of clothes: suit, shirt, underwear, socks and tie, shoes—having been required to take home every stitch of his clothing on that first day. As he dressed, I looked over the report of his hospitalization that Pierre had prepared. I would have to translate it for the New York doctors when we got home.

After settling up with the hospital—I wrote a final check for 2795 francs beyond the six payments of 2360 francs I had already made (after six days, the cashier had demanded no further payment, as Pierre's service, *médecine interne,* internal medicine, was much less expensive than the previous *chirurgie,* surgery)—after settling up with the hospital, we strolled up the rue du Faubourg-St-Jacques to the boulevard de Port-Royal. Ahead, just beyond the RER station was the Closerie des Lilas— once a haunt of Ernest Hemingway—where we would stop for lunch. George leaned back against the banquette, fingers toying with the stem of his water glass, aglow with the pleasure of being restored to his former life. The restaurant's connection with Hemingway only reinforced his sense that the world had come right. His company was Hemingway's publisher.

Pierre's report had urged a complete investigation of the heart, above all to determine whether George had a problem with arrhythmia. If he had suffered episodes of atrial fibrillation, a specific treatment would have to be determined so as to prevent *"accidents emboliques,"* embolismic accidents. That specter again. Heart attack. Or something equally threatening. But for the time being, I relaxed and reveled in George's presence, in his apparent vitality. We had been restored to one another. His care would be up to the American doctors now.

FITTING IN

When staying in my apartment in Paris, it was at one time my habit, before going home at night, to stop at a twenty-four-hour *pâtisserie* in the rue de l'Ancienne-Comédie to buy croissants for the following morning. Even as I turned into the street, I could see under the night sky the amber glow of the shop's open front, the light reflecting off the multi-level rows of lightly browned baked goods. It was a real convenience to be able to buy crisp, fresh croissants so late at night; it meant I wouldn't have to go out before breakfast the following day. Once at the shop, I would join the customers lined along the glass-enclosed counter that angled backward into the shop's interior space. The line moved quickly, as customer and clerk conducted their transactions in clipped, efficient tones. When, finally, it was my turn, I would try to be equally efficient: *"Deux croissants beurre, s'il vous plaît."* (I couldn't always get my words out as quickly as I wanted to.) The clerk would pluck two croissants from the tray and, with hand movements too quick to grasp, wrap them in a sheet of thin, crackly paper twisted tight at each end. *"Dix francs,"* he would say, extending an open palm. I would hand him my ten-franc piece and each time my secret thought would be: *I wonder if he thinks I'm French.*

When I bought the Paris apartment, I saw that as one of the possibilities: to fit in, to dissolve into Frenchness, to become, in some way, French. I had cherished since childhood that place inside myself that tied me to the language, the rightness I felt in the language despite the fact that, apart from a certain linguistic complicity with my mother, who used French words and phrases to communicate what she wanted only me to understand, most of my experience of the language was in school. I saw the apartment, above all, as a way of living in the language. After George's death of a heart attack only months after I bought it, it became clear that I would have to create my Paris self on my own.

My progress to that end was not without detours. Realizing after George died that I could no longer afford the New York apartment, I moved with our two cats—a massively dignified calico named Mariah and a ripsnorting ginger-and-white tiger named Murray—into an old farmhouse George had owned in rural New Jersey. The house was in need of immediate repairs—roof, porch, gutters, foundation walls, septic drain, but it was also full of George's presence. I clung to that presence, fed off it. A book about him practically poured out of me, a tribute and also a catharsis.

Shortly after the book was published, I returned to Pittsburgh to attend three Division Series games between the Pittsburgh Pirates and the Cincinnati Reds. Over the many summers I had spent in Pittsburgh with grandparents, being a fan of the Pirates had become a part of my identity, though I hadn't been to the city in years. The Pittsburgh I returned to was a city devastated by the decline of Big Steel. Again I felt the urge to write—about the drama of the industrial landscape and

what had been lost. In researching that book, on a tour of the Edgar Thomson Works of U.S. Steel, I met Bob. Two years later we were married.

Through those years, Paris was a focus, but not a single-minded one. I got there at least once a year, each time choosing a print for the apartment, an end table, a lamp. But once the Pittsburgh book was published, the Paris apartment loomed large again.

I didn't intend it as such, but the apartment, small as it is, is probably better as an apartment for one. I decorated its all-white interior in deep greens, with touches of mustard and more white. In the living room, over the sofa and on either side of the fireplace, hang botanical prints that I found in a shop in the place des Vosges. A Rothko poster in shades of yellow-green hangs above the desk in the small living-room alcove. The casement windows in living room and bedroom are framed by white tieback curtains with a *galon,* a ribbon border, again in deep tones of green. It is an unaccountably peaceful place. In bed late at night, under a duvet, I would put down my book and listen to the rhythms of the traffic, the throttling of a motorcycle up the rue de Condé, the approach of women's heels along the rue St-Sulpice, the bravado in the voices of young men, the joy in young women's laughter. The music of life. As the night deepened, the human presence would diminish, until by 4 a.m. there was only the hush of a city asleep. I was snug in my bed. What did I mean by "fitting in"? What did I want it to mean?

In his book *Paris,* published in 1983, the art critic John Russell describes the Parisian as "brisk, ironical, self-regarding, invalidish, mischievous, fickle, and dry." He goes on to say that, in contrast to the revolutions in manners that differentiate Elizabethan or Georgian England from today, "the wit, the intelligence, the enlightened materialism, and the spry, darting physique of the Parisian have not altered since the

Renaissance." Where did I fit into that? Although I had lived in New York and worked in publishing for nearly twenty years, I had spent the bulk of my childhood in Evanston, Illinois, and Pittsburgh, Pennsylvania. The men in my family tended to be lawyers or bankers or manufacturers, most notably of bolts and nuts. And even in sophisticated New York the wellspring of history was not deep.

    The business of vibrant, modern Paris functions within the landmarks of the city's history and culture. To walk the city's streets is to be enveloped almost palpably in history's associations. Even the first-time visitor feels a start of recognition, a sense of oneness at the mere sound of the words *Louvre, Eiffel Tower, Champs-Élysées, Arc de Triomphe, Luxembourg Gardens.* Who can walk past the Conciergerie, a prison as early as the fourteenth century, and not feel the despairing breaths of Marie Antoinette? Admire the obelisk, the fountains, the gilded lampposts of the place de la Concorde, without hearing the shhhhhhump of the guillotine blade? Layers of darkness exist even today in the failures of the French social model, well-intentioned in the abstract, less successful in application. The ideal of the social model is a balance between economic prosperity and social justice, but the result has been over-regulation and economic and social stagnation, not to mention a state in which minorities are often closed off from acceptance and opportunity. I am aware that my life in Paris is a privileged one.

    My building incorporates its own ambiguity, though I didn't learn the details of its history until after I bought the apartment. As the French count them, it is a building of five floors and a *rez-de-chaussée,* or ground floor, with apartments on either side of a circular central staircase, and little suggestion of its somewhat louche past. All the rooms were separate when it was built in the mid-seventeenth century as a small hotel—

respectable enough. But it is probable that it subsequently devolved into a *maison close,* or brothel, serving the priests and seminarians of nearby St-Sulpice. (My eyes popped when I received this bit of information.) Apparently, there were many such establishments along the street. Madame D, whose family knows the building intimately and now lives in the apartment above mine, tells of the former bars on the windows—for protection, presumably, but also to keep the women from sneaking out and the customers from sneaking in. Eventually, *des SDF (sans domicile fixe)*, or homeless, were finding refuge in the ground-floor hallway. The building's return to respectability proceeded only in stages, as it became, first, a *maison meublée,* or apartment hotel, and then was bought piece by piece by a single family. Today, divided into condominium apartments, it is quiet, comparatively pristine, and unreservedly *classe moyenne.*

I am a creature of habit. And so, on my early trips to Paris, I fell into routines, many of which I still adhere to. Routine can be embracing to me, a way to re-experience pleasure. I draw comfort from their repetition. Soon after my arrival, after getting settled, I would leave my apartment and round the corner of my narrow street into the airier expanse of the carrefour de l'Odéon, where, at the *papeterie,* or stationer's shop, I would choose the book that I would read during my stay. On a shelf toward the back, novels lay faceup in their pale paper covers, many with detachable red bands denoting the prize the book had won—Prix Goncourt, Prix Renaudot, Prix Femina, Prix Médicis. I would pick up each book in turn, reading the copy on the back cover, a page or two of the first chapter, looking for the novel whose subject would most appeal to me and whose vocabulary I could most easily manage. After I had made my purchase, the red band would make a convenient bookmark. The *papeterie* is still there in the *carrefour,* lodged between a *crêperie* and a costume shop. But the shelf that once held books now boasts additional stationery supplies. The *pâtisserie,* too, no longer exists. The building in which it was housed is undergoing significant renovations. Its disappearance taught me a lesson about permanence even in tradition-minded Paris. Now I have to stop in the Buci market by early evening, if I can get there in time, to buy my croissants.

 Of the routines that survive, the most longstanding is lunch on the day of my arrival at the Café de la Mairie in the place St-Sulpice, at the opposite end of the street from the *carrefour.* Or perhaps the routine begins even earlier, as the plane sets down at Charles de Gaulle around 7 a.m. and I taxi into central Paris to the apartment and immediately crawl into bed. Three hours later I awaken to the beep of my alarm clock, foggy and wiltingly hungry. I make my way up the rue St-Sulpice past restaurants and modish shops. Pale cream house fronts rise four or five stories above the ground-level *boutiques,* or commercial spaces, on either side of the narrow street. Weather permitting, flowers spill through the wrought-iron grilles at the windows; the windows themselves grow progressively smaller with each ascending floor above the piano nobile, or *étage noble.* On the left-hand side of the street, silhouetted against the sky, the north tower of St-Sulpice Church acts as a beacon drawing me forward.

 There is nothing attractive about the interior of the Café de la Mairie. It has the air most of all of a down-at-the-heels lunchroom, with harried waiters too few in number to achieve the French waiter's customary brisk grace. It is the rows of chairs and small tables in front of the café that account for its draw, the view of the *place* from under the trees: the columned façade of St-Sulpice Church, the mairie, or municipal headquarters, of the sixth *arrondissement* facing the church from across the square, the former seminary along the square's southern border, and at its center the punning Fontaine des Quatre Points Cardinaux. Also known as the Fontaine des Quatre-Évêques, the fountain acquired its more roguish name in a delicious exercise of French wit. Four sculpted bishops, each facing one of the four cardinal points, preside over the three-tiered fountain—Bossuet, Fénelon, Massillon, and Fléchier. None of the four was ever elevated to cardinal, hence the second meaning of *points cardinaux*—"never cardinals." The word *point* in French means both "point" and "never." (Strict grammarians might protest that in the latter interpretation, *point* would not have an "s.")

Other routines involve walking: through the Luxembourg Gardens, up the rue de l'Ancienne-Comédie and beyond to the Pont des Arts and the Louvre, to the place Vendôme or the Tuileries and the place de la Concorde. Or upriver from the Pont des Arts to Notre Dame and the Île St-Louis. A subtext on all these walks is the French artistry with flowers, the changing designs with each year, each season, patterns as fine as lace or bursting with color and panache. And not just in the major gardens. At any moment flowers may reveal themselves from around a corner: pansies and daisies bunched along a wrought-iron fence or building wall, tulips keeping company with an agèd tree, narcissus filling some otherwise undistinguished patch of earth. It was on one of these walks that I discovered, at a flower stall, that the word "pansy" is a corruption of the French word *"pensée,"* or thought.

Until it was closed for renovation, I made yearly visits to the Conservatoire des Arts et Métiers, home to the survivor of two steam vehicles built by Nicolas-Joseph Cugnot. Thought to be the first-ever self-propelled vehicle, Cugnot's artillery wagon (the museum's version dates to 1770), is a huge, primitive, lumbering affair with none of the finesse of steam cars to come. Nonetheless, I felt drawn to this ancestor of the bright-red

Stanley Steamer that George had given me shortly after we were married. In the new, renovated *Conservatoire,* Cugnot's *fardier à vapeur* has pride of place in a vaulting, white-walled room with a no-nonsense guard stationed nearby. When I leaned too close on a post-renovation visit, he cried out *"Madame, ne touchez pas!,"* shattering my composure and filling me with unwarranted guilt—I'd had no intention of touching it. When I think of the *Conservatoire,* which also houses numerous early automobiles, the plane in which Blériot crossed the Channel, Foucault's pendulum, and myriad other technological and industrial artifacts, I think of Gertrude Stein's observation in *Paris France:* "The reason why all of us naturally began to live in France is because France has scientific methods, machines and electricity, but does not really believe that these things have anything to do with the real business of living." Perhaps that is why these treasures have waited so long for a worthy, renovated home.

But any tourist can form routines. I wanted the identification to go further. I studied the women in my neighborhood, who, because it was so close to the Sorbonne, were disproportionately young. I particularly noticed the young ones, walking in their narrow black pants and their pert black jackets, their clunky black heels clacking on the pavement. I marveled over the narrowness of their hips, which seemed at times no more than ten inches wide. I am not heavy, but I felt totally outsized. How could they ever have children? And always there was a waist. I began to realize that, as much as the proverbial scarf, the waist was central to looking French, a focal point for the eye, not to be hidden by overblouses or long, loose sweaters—the sort of flowing lines that more or less made up my wardrobe.

Most difficult to pin down was the walk itself, clean, swift, like a knife slicing through air. Those women were the image of

authority and purpose. It was some time before I defined the walk to my satisfaction, watching them pass by, as I sat outside a café nursing an espresso. The key, I finally decided, was that they don't move their upper bodies. This was not the slouching, loose-limbed walk of many Americans. Their shoulders were erect and still. Even the hips moved very little. The walk was in the strong, quick, heel-clacking legs. And it was those erect shoulders that held a scarf in place.

This ability to remain physically within themselves, not to sprawl, to keep their upper bodies still, their elbows at their sides, is particularly evident—and useful—in the tight spaces of *bistros* or *cafés*. It is a containment I still haven't entirely mastered. Nonetheless, in all other respects that I can think of, and I know I'm not alone here, I was born to linger in a French café. In the main, a French café answers the needs of my personality: because the food comes quickly and at nearly any hour, because you can go there by yourself, because you can read in a culture biased toward reading, because I am a people-watcher, and because I enjoy the rhythm of the waitstaff dance. I relish the pfft! of *gaz* as my Perrier is opened, the paper placemat slapped onto the table, then unfolded, the metal basket of condiments, all delivered by the white-shirted, black-vested waiter as he, or nowadays she, pauses in mid-stride. I revere the staff's brisk politeness, their amazing competence, the smile that sneaks through the dignified professionalism.

Still, in all these respects, I am largely a spectator. There are ways in which I will never be French. Most significantly, I don't care enough about food. I once told an American friend who was married to a Frenchman and had studied at the Cordon Bleu cooking school that I didn't like to cook but loved to eat. She rose up all *froideur* and informed me that if you don't like to cook, you have no idea what it means to love to eat. I didn't even try to answer. I appreciate intellectually how food links the French to the land, to *terroir*, the subtle variations in flavor arising out of the nature of the soil. But I have neither the skill nor the temperament to spend the afternoon cutting and chopping in the preparation of perfect *petits plats*, or little dishes. I lack the formidable expertise of the shoppers I see in the Buci market, scrutinizing the fruits and vegetables, refusing the *boucher's* proffered cut of meat and insisting on something better. Even cats are entitled to at least the illusion of gourmet food. At one point I expected to bring my tiny Burmese with me on my trips to Paris. (I gave up the idea after hearing dark— and probably apocryphal—tales of immigration agents at JFK whisking cats away from their owners, never to be returned.) In anticipation, I bought several tins of Sheba cat food. Their flavors had the air of a restaurant menu: *Panache aux Gibiers, Terrine au Lapin, Duo au Foie et à la Volaille.*

If it was the language that brought me to Paris, it was largely the literary language, the language of Racine and Chateaubriand and Flaubert. I am not well versed in slang. One locution about covers it: *T'as du fric?*, Do you have any money? On the other hand, I don't talk that way in English either. Got any scratch? I still don't have certain instincts: *Ah bon,* for "I see, I understand," or interrogatively, *Ah bon?*, for "Oh, really?" Or that insistent, sibilant contradiction of a negative, *si si si!*, yes, yes, yes! I can't always depend on my French. Often enough, the words come out fluently, but at times I am nearly tongue-tied. Just after I made the offer on the apartment, Madame C, one of the real-estate agents I had been working with, invited me to lunch. She wasn't representing the apartment I had made the offer on; we had just had a good time together, chatting easily and amiably. But this time my brain couldn't frame the words. I sat guiltily at the table as she carried on virtually the entire conversation by herself.

The French are a fascinating combination of laborious

politeness and humor verging on the rude—at least to many non-French ears. Not for them the self-deprecating humor of the Anglo-Saxon, which they tend to disdain as unworthy, the manner of a loser. For them conversation is an art, a game of wit and one-upmanship, of philosophical reference and word-play. Who better to have coined the expression *l'esprit de l'escalier,* the wit of the staircase, the retort you don't think of until descending the staircase on your way home? I am a specialist in *l'esprit de l'escalier* even in English. Nor does the laborious politeness of the French come naturally to me. I remember meeting a French friend, a woman "of a certain age," for coffee at 10:30 one morning. We sat across from one another by the window at a small table for two. The restaurant was empty of customers apart from ourselves, but our attempts at conversation were rendered virtually inaudible by the music emanating from the sound system. As the waiter returned with our order, my friend launched into a full, elegant paragraph of entreaty—I am here with my friend whom I haven't seen in months, we would like to be able to converse comfortably, I realize that some people like their music louder than others, I don't mean to inconvenience anyone, I'm sure you will understand, if it is at all possible, would you be good enough, etc., etc.—all of which I would have reduced to: "Could you possibly turn the music down?" What the French aspire to is style.

    I did have some early moments of holding my own. The renovations on my apartment had for some reason not included an *applique,* or light fixture, for the light bulb drooping out of the hole above the living room door. I bought an *applique* of what I thought was the right size at one of the large department stores. But when I got it home, I discovered that it was much too big. What would any good American do? Return it of course. But when I got back to the store, the sales clerk was appalled. No one had ever asked to return something before—

FITTING IN

or so she would have me believe. You should have bought the right size to begin with, she said. I just stood there, not quite knowing what the problem was. No one had told me that returning merchandise is much less common in France. Finally, perhaps deeming it not worth the effort to try to reason with a foreigner, she took the *applique* and gave me the appropriate credit—her stony demeanor making it clear what an extraordinary gesture that was.

The same naïve stubbornness helped me out with the phone company. When the man from France Télécom came to install the phone, he didn't bring a phone book. It was up to me to pick one up at the phone company office somewhere near the Luxembourg Gardens. When I arrived, I was directed to a Dutch door, the top half of which was open. Inside was a dark-haired woman in a turquoise smock who stood only slightly taller than the bottom half of the door. When I told her I was there to pick up my phone book, she disappeared for a moment, then reappeared with several volumes—I hadn't realized that Paris phone books came as multivolume sets—that looked as though they had been put through a washer and dryer. I protested that those phone books had been wet. They'll still work perfectly well, she replied. I restated my case. She wouldn't budge. Neither would I. We stood on either side of the door, glowering at each other, until finally she gave in and found me phone books that had escaped the flood. I think it was time for her lunch.

But I could never match the triumph of my friend Barbara. Barbara had a date for dinner in Paris with a glamorous Frenchman. She is not a conventionally pretty woman, more what the French call *une belle-laide*, but I can imagine how striking she was in her little black dress, her face highlighted by billowing auburn hair and her immense personal warmth. At the last minute, her date called to cancel. There she was, all dressed up with nowhere to go. Refusing to be defeated, she gathered up her handbag and her Yorkshire terrier and set off for the Brasserie Lipp, the renowned haunt of France's political elite. The maître d' was suitably impressed. Rather than shunting her off to some ignominious Lippian hinterland, as he would most Americans, he treated her like royalty, seating her at a highly desirable table up front. When her dinner arrived, she asked the waiter if he could bring a *petit quelque chose pour le chien*—a little something for the dog. He returned from the kitchen with a selection of table scraps in a small silver bowl.

Not long ago I learned one of the most important keys to sounding French, an element of linguistic style that, without further analysis, I mistook simply for elegance. The eminent scholar and author Jacques Barzun calls it a different "turn of mind"—that is, the emphasis in French on the noun over the verb, of *l'être,* being, over *le processus,* process. As an example, Barzun writes in *An Essay on French Verse,* "if you want to say that someone has impeccable manners but is not very friendly, you can give the equivalent of each word in turn and you will be understood, but your sentence will not sound like real French. You must turn the thought and say: *"il est d'une parfaite courtoisie, mais il est peu abordable"*—literally, he is of a perfect courtesy, but he is not very approachable.

I have since made a habit of collecting examples of this French "turn of mind." The ATM machine at my bank in the States lets me choose the language in which I want to conduct my transaction. I always choose French, for the fun of it and to reinforce the case for including French on the ATM's list of languages—doing my bit for *la francophonie,* the presence of French on the world stage. After I have punched in my request, the machine asks me to be patient. *"Votre opération,"* the screen reads, *"est en cours d'exécution."* In English we would say, "Your transaction is being processed." Similarly, a recent exhibition of photographs of the Gobi Desert displayed along the fence of the Luxembourg Gardens included an image of women planting straw in their struggle against the desert's advance. According to the photograph's label, the straw was intended to stabilize the sand and to capture some moisture *"pour permettre la pousse d'épineux."* The label's English translation gave more prominence to the verb—"to enable a few thorny plants to grow." The secondary status of the verb in French is nowhere more evident than with such verbs as *avoir, mettre, donner, faire,* as in *faire la chambre, faire l'argenterie, faire la vitrine, faire un poème, faire peur*— make up the room, polish the silver, dress the window, write a poem, scare. The do-all verb leaves it to the noun to define.

Curiously, in another French turn of mind, the reflexive verb, the verb is strengthened. Barzun offers the following example: *le plat se mange arrosé de citron*—the dish is served with lemon juice. Here *se mange,* though passive in sense, is actually in the active voice; *is served,* the English equivalent, is in the weaker passive. Such use of the reflexive verb is another key to sounding French. Often enough, I find myself asking, *Ça se prononce comment?*— How is that pronounced? Or *Ça se dit comment?*—What is the word for that? (literally, How is that said?). And both the emphasis on the noun and the reflexive verb do add the notes of elegance that I once thought were the whole story.

The French emphasis on the noun is pushed to its ultimate extreme in *Le Train de Nulle Part*—*The Train from Nowhere,* published in 2004 and billed as the first novel without verbs. The novel's dedication is a mock-hysterical (one assumes) call to arms to *"tous les farouches ennemis du verbe"*—all fierce enemies of the verb, *"cet envahisseur, ce dictateur, cet usurpateur de notre littérature depuis toujours!"*-- this invader, this dictator, this usurper of our literature from the very beginning! The tale of a train ride among passengers portrayed in scabrous detail, the novel by Michel Thaler, whose name in fact is Michel Dansel, consists of 233 pages of sentence fragments—a flood of nouns, adverbs, adjectives (and past participles used as adjectives), peppered with exclamation points. Reviews in both the French- and English-speaking press, more than one of them verbless, have not been kind. The French magazine *Lire* called the novel "a bad paper by an 11-year-old student." And although I abhor the thought of being one of those "bourgeois" who would ban Flaubert's *Madame Bovary* or Baudelaire's *Les Fleurs du Mal*, I find it hard to admire such imagery as *"sa voix de fosse d'aisance en action"*—her voice like a cesspool in action; or *"son mâle en pleine tétée,"* her male greedily sucking, *"un nichon bleuâtre en forme de demi-pastèque talée dans la truffe"*—a bluish boob in the shape of a watermelon-half squashed into his snout. And the air of inertia resulting from the lack of verbs means the reader can't escape!

    I sometimes wonder if people are different according to the language they speak, whether certain structures of the language or its music might have an influence on their behavior, beyond the deeper commonalities we all share. I know it's been a much debated topic. I once posed the question to Steven Pinker, the renowned cognitive scientist and former student of Noam Chomsky. He told me he couldn't even begin to answer that. (I confess I asked him at a cocktail reception before he was to give a talk, admittedly not the ideal time.) But I think, for example, about the fact that French emphasizes the noun over the verb, being over process. Does this have something to do with the way the French sink into the moment, into the sensual, into aesthetic pleasure? Does it have something to do with their tendency to savor their food, to eat slowly, all five senses attuned? In *Au Contraire!*, Gilles Asselin and Ruth Mastron write that "friends in France may…share activities or tasks, but they

FITTING IN

do not always feel the need to do so; simply being together is enough. This reflects the French cultural orientation toward being. A group of friends may get together with no particular purpose in mind. During their time together they may discuss possibilities....The discussing is more important than the doing." And although it manifests itself more fully in the literary than the spoken language, does the flow of the language—the lack of strong accent, the resonant vowels smoothly linked by liaison—do its own part in drawing one into the moment? Surely it has something to do with the efficacy of the art of seduction!

Or could it be, on the contrary, that it is a people's identity that accounts for linguistic style? Is that simply unanswerable? Will we ever know enough about a language's origins? We might as easily try to resolve the question of the chicken and the egg. But regardless of how it was formed, the language could still shape behavior. There's no denying that, for most of us, when we were born the language was already there.

Am I different in French? On some level I think I might be. In my apartment one morning, an American friend listened in as I asked Madame D myriad questions about the building. Once Madame D had left, she exclaimed over how different I was when I spoke French. "You did much more with your hands," she said. "You embellished things with your hands, expressed emotion with your hands. Your face was more expressive, especially when you were listening. When you were talking, your voice was lighter." Another American friend was not so positive. "You speak French too fast," she said. "Faster than you speak English. You're not being yourself." I retorted that that's just the way it came out, but I don't think she was satisfied with my reply.

I even surprised myself as I boarded a post - 9/11 flight to the States at Charles de Gaulle. My daughter-in-law had urged me to take pictures of the Paris apartment, which she had never seen. Fearing that the x-ray machine would damage the photographs, I attempted to carry my disposable camera through security. When the security official told me to lay the camera on the belt, I refused, protesting that the photographs would be ruined. He repeated his order, more forcefully this time. Again I refused. When he told me a third time, I heard myself cry out, in a voice an octave higher than its usual range, *"J'insiste!"* I stood there defiantly, arms akimbo, all righteous indignation. Other passengers stared. I can't even imagine myself behaving that way in English. Fortunately, in a Latin country such eruptions are not uncommon. At least I believe that's the reason I got away with it. When the security official insisted again—*"C'est moi qui insiste!"* he declared—in a tone that indicated the debate was over, I gave up and put the camera on the belt. At any U.S. airport I would long since have been hauled off to some isolated back room. But here I was in the language and I did what the language would do. It all proved unnecessary. The pictures came through unharmed.

Could I live in Paris? Amid all this style, all this perfection, in this civilization so much older and more complex than my own? I think of Giovanni in James Baldwin's *Giovanni's Room*. Told that the French consider Italians too fluid, too volatile, with no sense of measure, he cries out in protest, "Measure! Ah, these people and their measure…and what do they get out of all this measure?" Exquisiteness, one could answer. But I know what he means. One incident in particular makes me fear I am irredeemably American. In 1996 the Pittsburgh Steelers were playing the Dallas Cowboys in the Super Bowl. By this time I had moved from New York to Pittsburgh, my family's home for generations, and I had caught some of the city's excitement over the Steelers. Learning that the game would be shown in Paris on cable (I was in Paris during the week the game was to be played), I went from one to another of the small hotels in my neighborhood, thinking I could reserve a room for the night (I had no television in the apartment). But none of the hotels had cable. I didn't think the game worth the price of some place like the Hôtel de Crillon, which probably did have cable, so I resigned myself to listening to the game on BBC radio. That night, after turning out the lights, I lay in bed, with the radio at my side, waiting for the game to start. I listened to the traffic in the street below, the footsteps on the sidewalk, feeling the tie to home. When they played the "Star Spangled Banner," I burst into tears.

Still, in my own way, I have come over the years to fit in—not as much, I think, by conscious effort as by the subtle accretion of experience. Since buying the apartment, I have tried to get to Paris for a week or two, at least once or twice a year, some years even more often. The last time I was there, I dressed for the most part in black: turtleneck, trousers, hip-length leather jacket. My hair was cut short. The scarf at my neck was a reproduction of a design for stained glass by the American artist John La Farge. As I walked, people in the street—even French people—asked me repeatedly for directions. I felt such ease, answering when I could, offering apologies when I could not. Isn't that part of fitting in—ease? Forgetting you are not in your home place? I have never tried to establish an extensive social life among the French. I think I've always been afraid that, if I did, I would be too close to see the Paris of my imagination, that I would lose my ability to see the city fresh, that the city might simply dissolve into the background. That transcendent, beautiful place of language made manifest. Yet, what I have there feeds me profoundly. I have learned what I meant by "fitting in." I have fit in to my dream of Paris. For me that is enough. I think I have what I wanted.

CONNECTIONS

I LIKE TO TELL PEOPLE THAT I HAVE TWO CITIES —Paris and Pittsburgh. The alliteration pleases me, of course, but most of all it is the look of befuddlement on my listeners' faces that tickles me. I relish the start of surprise, the knot of perplexity between the eyebrows, the tentative wry smile at the incongruity of it. Pittsburgh—conservative, inward-looking, the butt of jokes for its soot-filled past versus Paris—world capital, sophisticated, a composite of architecture and *art de vivre* that makes it the stuff of dreams. The two cities are not often mentioned in the same breath. On the face of it, their conjoining in even one mind seems improbable. One wonders where they could even intersect.

And yet they do, in ways both incidental and profound. Most people are familiar with the architecture, the shapes and colors of Paris. They are much less so of Pittsburgh. They do not know that, like Paris, Pittsburgh is a visual feast. Cradled in formerly smoke-blighted, now verdant hills, centered on the junction of two great rivers, Pittsburgh is a symphony of geometrical shapes—the triangles of gables, of spires of skyscrapers, the rectangles of nineteenth- and early twentieth-century house fronts, the domes of churches, the leaping arcs of bridges, all tightly clustered in deference to the terrain. Looking out over the city from the bluff above the confluence of the rivers, I think of the woodcuts of the medieval cities of Europe in such incunabula as the *Nuremburg Chronicle*. In the downtown towers, the house fronts spilling over the hills, I see the same foreshortening of buildings set close, the same congruity of line, the same sense of oneness with the landscape. As in Paris, streets in Pittsburgh are often narrow, joining at odd angles, their routes erratic. Like the Seine, Pittsburgh's rivers—the Allegheny, the Monongahela, and the Ohio—are working as well as pleasure rivers. In both cities, skies are changeable, often gray. Pittsburgh is set, in fact, on land the French once claimed as their own, building in 1754, at the confluence of the rivers, the tiny earth and timber fort they called Fort Duquesne.

Nonetheless, Pittsburgh is a quintessential industrial, or post-industrial, American city. The making of steel still lingers in its self-image. Some residential neighborhoods still hug industrial structures. From my window on the bluff, I look down on coal barges tied up along the near bank of the Monongahela, as it joins the Allegheny to form the Ohio. Railroad tracks line the flats along the "Mon." Skyscrapers of steel, aluminum, and glass rise from the triangle of land at the junction of the rivers, their shimmering tops scarcely higher than eye level from my vantage point on the bluff. The trusses and cables of nineteen bridges anchor the city in multifarious rhythms. The grit of the real predominates here. I feel drawn to the city's raw edge.

In the back and forth between Pittsburgh and Paris, I have come to enjoy traveling around Pittsburgh putting French names to things, feeling the slight shift in connotation such an exercise brings. From where I stand on the *falaise,* bluff, I see *collines,* hills, *verdure,* greenery, *rivières* or *fleuves,* rivers, *bateaux* à vapeur, steamboats, péniches, barges, filled with charbon, coal. Au coucher du soleil, at sunset, I see the lueur, glow, of rose-colored light reflected in the cladding of the gratte-ciel, skyscrapers. In the old days, breezes wafted la suie, soot, emanating from the aciéries, steel mills.

When I drive around Pittsburgh, with its falaises, fleuves, collines, I sometimes think of Chateaubriand's transcendent descriptions of American wilderness. Chateaubriand traveled to le nouveau monde in 1791, and, according to Louis Desgraves's introduction to my own copy of Chateaubriand's René, made it as far as the confluence of the Ohio and the Mississippi. One passage from Chateaubriand's novel speaks in particular to my understanding of Western Pennsylvania and my home place, just west of the Appalachians, at the headwaters of the Ohio. René stands at dawn on the bank of the Mississippi with his adoptive father, Chactas, a sachem among the Natchez, and le père Souël, a missionary at the nearby Fort Rosalie. *"Vers l'orient,"* Chateaubriand writes, *"au fond de la perspective, le soleil commençoit à paroître entre les sommets brisés des Apalaches, qui se dessinoient comme des caractères d'azur dans les hauteurs dorées du ciel; à l'occident, le Meschacebé rouloit ses ondes dans un silence magnifique, et formoit la bordure du tableau avec une inconcevable grandeur."*—"To the east, at the distant horizon, the sun began to rise between the broken summits of the Appalachians, which were outlined like letters of azure in the golden heights of the sky. To the west, the waves of the Mississippi rolled on in a magnificent silence and edged the vista with an inconceivable grandeur." The untranslatable music of the French makes the scene as stirring as a Bierstadt or a Thomas Cole painting, suffused with a comparable, mythic light.

It is the music of French words that accounts in large part for the shift in connotation as I put French names to things. With their extended vowels and muted consonants, they have a softening effect. They seem to encapsulate the beauty of *collines, verdure, fleuves,* humanize the utilitarian *péniches, charbon, aciéries.* There is something in the way the words themselves, the alluring vowels, draw at the heart in a way that English does less often (I can't forget that signal exception—"cellar door"). I feel an added layer of attachment, a heightened intimacy with the object the French word signifies. It's almost as though French words have love for the object in them. Admittedly, the French equivalents are not always lyrical. A bridge girder, for example, translates to *poutre métallique.* For me, there are few words harder to pronounce than *poutre,* with that uvular "r" coming after the "t" and before the mute "e." Still, it is difficult to imagine how raw industrial landscapes could grow up in a world of such preponderantly gentle words—although of course they have. (At least the French tend not to put them in the center of town.) In the end, Pittsburgh jibes more fully with the straightforward bluntness of English.

So, my two cities, one formed by a civilizing aesthetic (at least theoretically) and an aspiration to grandeur, the other an outgrowth of often physical, even heroic work. Each has its own beauty, its own authenticity. And although Pittsburgh is much younger, it too is informed by history. There is substance here, because of the work, because of the mix of ethnic traditions, because of the dreams of the people who have lived here and their struggle for a good life. What the cities share, in the deepest sense, is character—one lofty, the other down-to-earth. And each lives through a language that reflects it.

For all of that, one can experience suggestions of the industrial at the center of Paris. In a visit to *les égouts,* for example, the sewers. Or to the Eiffel Tower, an engineering marvel with its filigree of *fer puddlé,* "puddled" or wrought iron, and its 2.5 million rivets. It ultimately escaped demolition thanks to the importance of its antennae to French radio tele-

graphy. It wasn't until some years after I bought my Paris apartment that I actually went up into the tower—with my husband Bob not long after we were married. Bob never did quite take to Paris, though he came to regard it with tolerance. As a foreman in a steel mill, he never quite lost the feeling that the French were mincing and ineffectual. The happiest day we spent there was a quasi-industrial one. It began as we followed a working barge along the Canal St-Martin, with its nine locks and tree-lined banks, south from the Place de Stalingrad to the square Frédéric Lemaître. We watched rapt as water rose and fell in the locks, walked in step with the slow, steady progress of the barge. One roadbed, carrying vehicular traffic over the canal, simply rotated to the side ninety degrees, nestling into the canal edge, to allow the barge to pass. It seemed impossible that the large hunk of street could fit back into place between the canal's banks. "They certainly know how to work in tight spaces," Bob exclaimed, in a momentary concession of respect.

The afternoon found us walking above the trees, literally, along an inspired example of industrial reuse—the nearly three-mile stretch of the Promenade Plantée. Once the roadbed of an elevated railway, extending from the Bastille to the Bois de Vincennes, the top of the viaduct has been transformed by arbors and flowers, benches and trellises into a walkway/park. How uncanny it was, alternately striding and lingering *en plein air* along a seemingly endless line of garden, then peering down at the street below or across, over treetops, at the windows of apartments on the upper floors. It left us lightheaded, exuberant. Still, in spite of Bob's pleasure, on most of my trips to Paris I've been there on my own.

I think it's in part the Latinate quality of the language that makes French so appeal to me, those words big in meaning, that tendency to abstraction that suits the Platonist in me. Since reading *The Republic* in college, I have happily accepted the idea

of the chair—chair as idea—dancing in eternal perfection independent of my mind. Jacques Barzun points out in his *Essay on French Verse* that "French is not double like English, but single." He points to the second, Latinate word in English that parallels the Anglo-Saxon derivative, as in "tool" and "instrument," "strength" and "fortitude," "land" and "territory," "quick" and "rapid," "motherhood" and "maternity." He goes on to explain that "such pairs are not exact duplicates; usually, the sense of the Latin derivative is more abstract or lofty." It occurs to me that French does have the word *"outil"* for "tool," as well as the word *"instrument,"* but that the larger point still holds: the Latinate word tends to be more resonant than the Anglo-Saxon derivative, and this figures in the relative effects of the two languages.

As illustration, take for example the famous couplet from Racine's Phèdre, part of *Phèdre's* agonized cry against the illicit passion that has possessed her:

> *"Ce n'est plus une ardeur dans mes veines cachée:*
> *C'est Vénus tout entière à sa proie attachée."*

Now read the same lines in Richard Wilbur's translation:

> *"Love hides no longer in these veins, at bay:*
> *Great Venus fastens on her helpless prey."*

Granted, poetry is largely untranslatable. On the other hand, Richard Wilbur is himself a poet. But that is not the issue here. The point is that the word "love" lacks the heat and fire of the Latinate *"ardeur."* Ardor, fervor, intensity, zeal, passion. The admittedly Latinate "passion" might be most nearly equivalent to *ardeur*, but is risky in this context, diminished as it is by profligate overuse. The English "ardor" bespeaks for me more crusading knights than erotic desire, and can never, in any event, match the sinuousness of the French *"ardeur,"* with its soft *"d"* and its extended *"eur."* The poet Ted Hughes, in his more contemporary translation, a translation more colloquial in feel, gives us perhaps the best word: "fever" (also Latinate). Similarly, in the second line, Wilbur's "Great Venus" is not as big as *Vénus tout entière.* We have the word "entire" in English, but it would be hard to make it work in this context. Hughes avoids the job of finding an adjective, investing the force of Venus in another noun, rendering the line as: "Venus has fastened on me like a tiger." But on the whole, Hughes's translation lacks the majesty of the French original.

Turning things around, I page through a bilingual edition of Hemingway's *The Old Man and the Sea.* The opening of one sentence in particular catches my eye:

"The speed of the line was cutting his hands badly...."

On the facing page, in a translation by Jean Dutourd of the Académie Française, the line reads:

"La ligne, dans sa furieuse galopade, lui écorchait cruellement les mains...."

For me, the French version is more vivid and intense, with its *"furieuse galopade,"* literally, "furious gallop" for "speed," and its "écorchait cruellement," literally, "cruelly tearing the skin," for "cutting...badly." (It is also more accurate. In the English version "speed" is the subject of the sentence. But it wasn't speed that was cutting his hands, it was the line. In the French version, it is *la ligne,* in its furious gallop, that does the cutting.)

On another page Hemingway speaks of "the evening breeze." In the French translation, the term is rendered *"la brise vespérale."* Imagine terse, "manly" Hemingway using a term like "vesperal breeze." There is no denying that French translated literally into English can become "purple," at least to an English-speaker's ear. The Latinate quality of the language is partly responsible, those big, lofty words. But there is also no doubt that the French prize extended rhetorical flights. And with a vowel language like French, a language of liaison and elision, uninterrupted by the minute stops that the more dominant consonants bring to English, they can really make it flow. I think of the Artists' Protest, *la Protestation des Artistes,* against the building of the Eiffel Tower, a portion of which can be found on the Eiffel Tower's official Web site (although I have chosen an example from the past, one can find such flights in any newspaper today):

> "Nous venons, écrivains, peintres, sculpteurs, architectes, amateurs passionnés de la beauté jusqu'ici intacte de Paris, protester de toutes nos forces, de toute notre indignation, au nom du goût français méconnu, au nom de l'art et de l'histoire français menacés, contre l'érection, en plein cœur de notre capitale, de l'inutile et monstrueuse Tour Eiffel, que la malignité publique, souvent empreinte de bon sens et d'esprit de justice, a déjà baptisée du nom de tour de Babel."

("We come, we writers, painters, sculptors, architects, lovers of the beauty of Paris which was until now intact, to protest with all our strength and all our indignation, in the name of the underestimated taste of the French, in the name of French art and history under threat, against the erection in the very heart of our capital, of the useless and monstrous Eiffel Tower, which popular ill-feeling, so often an arbiter of good sense and justice, has already christened the Tower of Babel.")

The Web site is a gold mine of delicious bombast, not necessarily lacking in specificity. Léon Bloy called the Tower *"ce lampadaire véritablement tragique,"* this truly tragic street lamp. François Coppée referred to *"ce mât de fer aux durs agrès,"* this mast of iron gymnasium apparatus." Maupassant called it *"cette haute et maigre pyramide d'échelles de fer, squelette disgracieux et géant,"* this high and skinny pyramid of iron ladders, this giant, ungainly skeleton. J-K Huysmans dubbed it *"un tuyau d'usine en construction,"* a half-built factory pipe. I should add that, once the tower was completed, most of the criticism fell away in the face of popular acclaim.

Journalists waxed eloquent over the tower's construction process. Émile Goudeau wrote in 1889, *"Une épaisse fumée de goudron et de houille prenait à la gorge, tandis qu'un bruit de ferraille rugissant sous le marteau nous assourdissait"*—"A thick cloud of tar and coal smoke seized the throat, and we were deafened by the din of metal screaming beneath the hammer." The workers, high on the structure, striking the rivets, setting off showers of sparks, *"avaient l'air de faucher des éclairs dans les nuées,"*—"looked as if they were reaping lightning bolts in the clouds." English, too, is capable of such heights. As recently as 1942, Marcia Davenport wrote in *The Valley of Decision,* which is set in Pittsburgh, of the drama of a Bessemer blow: "Element grappled with element, oxygen in a death-struggle with carbon, a battle more terrible and wonderful than man had ever made before. The flame, steady and fearfully red, began to change color, a descending scale of blinding flashes echoing from the death-and-birth agony of the elements. Inside the beast steel was being born." It was the work of Pittsburgh past, though portrayed in a style too flowery for this non-sentimental age.

CONNECTIONS

Are French words more magical? Is that where part of the appeal of the language lies? Surely some of them are. Some French words or expressions incorporate an intimacy with process, an observation or encapsulation of life, that brings an unexpected specificity and attentiveness to a language reputed for its abstraction. The mathematician Jean-Pierre Bourguignon compares the English and French terms for "cell phone." He writes that while the English speak of a cellular or cell, referring to the telephone's technology, the French most often speak of a *"portable,"* accentuating "the magical character of the object." (It should be noted that the term "mobile" is common among some English-speakers, though the term "cellular" or "cell" seems to prevail in the U.S.)

I have my own favorite magical words. Two of them begin with the physicality of the hand: *maintenant,* meaning "now," and *main courante,* meaning "hand rail." The "now" of *maintenant* is the immediate, personalized "what is held in the hand," from *main,* hand, and *tenant,* holding. It is the present drawn close. *Main courante,* or "running hand," calls intimately to mind the feel of holding, the movement of the hand along the rail of the banister as one climbs or descends the stairs. There are many others. *Tournesol,* sunflower, from the Italian *tornasole* (from *tornare,* turn, and *sole,* sun), capturing those big, brave brown and yellow faces following the sun. *Coucher du soleil,* the sun going to bed. *Gratte-ciel,* again, meaning skyscraper. The word gains something in its translation "from the American," in the verb *gratter,* which to my mind moves beyond "scraping" to the more closely defined act of scratching. I see fingers, fingernails, scratching the sky.

Shortly after I bought my apartment in Paris, I received a letter from the woman I had engaged to look after it while I was away. She had noticed *un éclat d'émail* in the bathtub, "a chip in the enamel," probably caused by the contractor who had been making additional renovations. *Éclat d'émail.* I couldn't resist the expression, the euphony of it, the burst or flash implicit in the word *éclat.* I've never forgotten it, *éclat d'émail.* On the other hand, I've just learned *nid-de-poule,* literally hen's nest. It means "pothole."

There is, admittedly, a downside to the Latinate quality of the language. In *Shakespeare and the French Poet,* Yves Bonnefoy, a distinguished literary figure and poet, as well as a translator of Shakespeare, observes that while French poetry is more about idea, essence, English poetry deals more with the diversity of the real. He attributes the failure of early translations of Shakespeare into French to the translators' attempts to mold Shakespeare into their own concepts of prosody and tragedy. He cites in particular "that facile and totally unpoetical alexandrine which was then the principal cause of the vapidity in the theater"—surely an overstatement on a par with throwing the baby out with the bathwater. Shakespeare, he says, captures universals through the empirical observation of people as they actually exist; Racine, by stripping situations and feelings "of all the contingent or accidental details of real life,...seems to raise them to the dignity of the Platonic Idea."

In its empirical approach, English is assisted by its short, blunt Anglo-Saxon words that zero in on the object without a larger resonance that can pull the reader away from the thing itself. And, for me, it's not just that the Latinate words are bigger, but that their euphony, the way they flow, tends to carry the reader off toward the ether. English, of course, has its own Latinate words. But, Bonnefoy says, these serve to "grant a more abstract handling of experience to an intelligence shaped by this 'devotion to the realm of things.'"

Even I have to admit to one area in which French is for the most part inadequate: baseball. Partly because French lacks snap. But also because of the elegance of those Latinate words and, often, the near impossibility of torturing French into an English-speaker's mindset. The Montreal Expos were kind enough years ago to send me a list of baseball terms with their English equivalents. I regard it as one of my treasures. Some French baseball terms are straightforward: *balle,* ball; *balle courbe,* curve ball; *double,* double; *erreur,* error; *coureur,* runner; *but volé,* stolen base; *billet,* ticket; *uniforme,* uniform. Others come from a higher elevation: *feinte illégale* or *irrégulière,* balk; *rectangle de l'instructeur,* coach's box; *intercepteur,* cut-off man; *abri des joueurs,* dugout; *choix de l'intérieur* or *optionnel,* fielder's choice; *retrait systématique,* force-out; *casque protecteur,* helmet; *coup en flèche,* line drive; *balle tombante,* sinker; *balle mouillée,* spitball; *piste d'avertissement,* warning track. It is hard to imagine sitting in the stands and chatting about the game in this vocabulary (though some terms, no doubt, get abbreviated, given the French-speaker's tendency to lop syllables off the ends of certain words when speaking informally—think *"ado"* for *adolescent, "sympa"* for *sympathique*). On a weekend trip to Montreal for a three-game series between les Pirates de Pittsburgh and les Expos de Montréal, I heard the Montreal radio announcer warn: *"Il faut se méfier de Womack* [the Pirates' second baseman], *il est rapide"*—You have to watch Womack, he's fast. The statement is comical—at least to an English-speaker—with its outsize *"se méfier"* and *"rapide."*

But even in baseball there are exceptions that are almost poetic: *frappe-et-court,* hit and run; *chandelle,* literally "candle," for pop fly; *risque-tout,* literally "risk everything," for squeeze play; *coup retenu,* literally "blow or hit held back," for bunt. With the word *"retenu,"* you can almost feel the gentle tap, the dulling reversal in the trajectory of the ball. The terms *"frappe-et-court"* and *"risque-tout"* could almost be said to have snap. And then there is *voltigeur* for outfielder, too Latinate, or more accurately Italianate, for words. The term *voltigeur* denotes a person who leaps from one galloping horse to another, an acrobat on the flying trapeze, one who vaults, leaps, bounds. A lovely image for an outfielder. Now that the Montreal Expos have become the Washington Nationals, all this French will have to be sustained by an independent-league team like the Capitales de Québec, or by the many amateur teams not only in French-speaking Canada but in France.

    At dinner one evening at La Méditerranée, the renowned fish restaurant in the place de l'Odéon, I was brought up short about Yves Bonnefoy. Seated to my left was a woman chicly dressed in black, a native English-speaker, who teaches Shakespeare at a French university. I mentioned Bonnefoy and his belief that French translations, and perhaps even the language itself, were inadequate to Shakespeare's achievement. "I know what Bonnefoy says," she countered. "But you have to look at the more recent translations by Jean-Michel Déprats." On returning to the States a few days later—I hadn't had a chance to look for them in Paris—I ordered the Déprats translations of *Hamlet* and *Richard II* from Amazon.fr. It seemed clear, after comparing the French and English versions of some of the most familiar speeches, that Déprats's translations are more "word-for-word" than others I have seen, show more effort to choose the strongest French word, more effort to capture the rhythm and flow of the Shakespearean line. He partakes of what Bonnefoy calls the comparative liberty of English poetry. In so doing, he perhaps comes closer to fulfilling Bonnefoy's own sense of the possibility inherent in the contemporary (c. 1962) "denial of idealism" in French poetry and the "surpassing of classical forms." Nowadays, the rules have fallen away. As Jacques Barzun points out, there is no longer only one style for poets collectively. He adds, though, that even now the alexandrine and other French meters are used more often than not.

CONNECTIONS

Shakespeare's poetry survives in many a Déprats line. As soon as the package from France arrived, I dropped everything to open its corrugated cardboard wrap and extract the two pocket paperback volumes. First one and then the other, I pored through each and, although aware that a translation can hardly be judged by a mere handful of lines, searched for signature passages.

The Ghost to Hamlet:

> "I am thy father's spirit,
> Doom'd for a certain term to walk the night,..."

Déprats's rendering reads:

> "*Je suis l'esprit de ton père,*
> *Condamné pour un temps à arpenter la nuit,...*"

It is a reasonably literal translation, but what sets it apart in particular is the flow of the phrase "*à arpenter la nuit*"—to pace the night. There is an openness to it, a vulnerability, born of the downward glide of the remainder of the line from the height of the "*ar*" in "*arpenter.*" (There is also a hiatus—the sort of hiccup-like pause—between the two vowels, the "*à*" followed by the "*a*" of "*arpenter,*" which no strict neoclassicist would condone.) Also notable is the vividness of the verb itself—*arpenter*—the back and forth, the anxiety in pacing. But above all there is much of the music of Shakespeare's lines. As Bonnefoy points out, many early translators of Shakespeare into French turned to rhapsody, or at least something little more than oratory, to capture higher or essential meanings at the expense of specificity and fidelity to Shakespeare's sound.

Hamlet to the players:

139

"*Dites cette tirade, je vous prie, comme je l'ai prononcée, lestement sur la langue;...*"

("Speak the speech, I pray you, as I pronounc'd it to you, trippingly on the tongue;...")

There is the same lift in intonation, the same lightness in "trippingly" and *"lestement."*
And the most famous speech of all:

"*Être, ou ne pas être, telle est la question.
Est-il plus noble pour l'esprit de souffrir
Les coups et les flèches d'une injurieuse fortune,
Ou de prendre les armes contre une mer de tourments,
Et, en les affrontant, y mettre fin?*"

("To be, or not to be, that is the question.
Whether 'tis nobler in the mind to suffer
The slings and arrows of outrageous fortune,
Or to take arms against a sea of troubles,
And, by opposing, end them.")

The French translation achieves a measure of the English staccato, of its poetry, and I am struck most of all by the cleanness, the finality, how much like the original is Déprats's rendering of the final line—how the words *"en les affrontant"* propel the line towards the curt, impenetrable *"fin."* It seems to me, in general, that the prominent consonants in English keep the movement of a line upright—like Roman type. In spite of the traditional equilibrium of the French poetic line, I see its movement, eased by soft consonants and by elision and liaison, as more forward-tending, more italic. It is also interesting to note, in connection with the "To be, or not to be" speech, an instance in which Bonnefoy seems right about early translations of Shakespeare into French. He cites the opening lines of Voltaire's translation:

> "*Demeure, il faut choisir, et passer à l'instant
> De la vie à la mort et de l'être au néant...*"

The words here mean literally:

> "Stay, you must choose, and move to the moment
> Of life unto death and being to naught."

(An alternate translation of the word *"Demeure,"* treating *"Demeure"* as a noun rather than as the imperative form of the verb *"demeurer,"* would be "dwelling, state of being.") Bonnefoy blames this "travesty of Shakespeare" on the alexandrine itself. Still one can't help but feel that more might have been accomplished within the alexandrine's confines.

What, I wondered, would Déprats make of my favorite lines from *Richard II*? I leafed through the pages, Act II, Scene 1, to find Jean de Gand—John of Gaunt:

> "*Ce noble trône de rois, cette île porteuse de sceptres,
> Terre de majesté, résidence de Mars,
> Cet autre Éden, ce demi-paradis,
> Cette forteresse bâtie par la Nature pour elle-même.
> Contre la contagion et la main de la guerre,
> Cette heureuse race d'hommes, ce petit univers,
> Cette pierre précieuse sertie dans une mer d'argent,
> Qui fait pour elle office de rempart,
> Ou de douve défendant la maison,*

IN OTHER WORDS

Contre la jalousie de pays moins heureux;
Cette parcelle bénie, cette terre, ce royaume,
  cette Angleterre,..."

("This royal throne of kings, this sceptred isle,
This earth of majesty, this seat of Mars,
This other Eden, demi-paradise,
This fortress built by Nature for herself
Against infection and the hand of war,
This happy breed of men, this little world,
This precious stone set in a silver sea,
Which serves it in the office of a wall,
Or as a moat defensive to a house,
Against the envy of less happier lands;
This blessed plot, this earth, this realm, this England,...")

Again, a literal translation, with lines of varying lengths. French seldom achieves the concision of English, but what is here is an openness at the ends of the lines, a flow, particularly in the second half of the line, that mimics Shakespeare's sound. Individual lines do not hold themselves in classic French equilibrium. Even one of the lines most handicapped by the language's lack of crispness—*"Cette forteresse bâtie par la Nature pour elle-même"*—recreates in *"par la Nature pour elle-même"* the forward drive of "by Nature for herself." (I have to admit that *"cette île porteuse de sceptres"* for "this sceptred isle" is less successful. Some nouns have adjectival forms in French, but *sceptre* isn't one of them.) Somehow, when close to Gaunt's speech, I hear an echo of a sonnet by Joachim du Bellay (c. 1522-1560), and in particular its first line: *"Heureux qui, comme Ulysse, a fait un beau voyage"*—"Happy he who, like Ulysses, has journeyed far." The music of Du Bellay's line calls to mind the English "This blessed plot, this earth, this realm, this England."

The half-line *"a fait un beau voyage"* recalls in particular the feel of *"de pays moins heureux."* Du Bellay predates Malherbe and the neoclassic codification of the rules of vocabulary and prosody. He is also one of many exemplars of the heights achieved in a poetic tradition often deemed stifled.

There are probably always exceptions when measuring the efficacy and aura of a language. The mellifluousness of French, the length and size of the words all make it more difficult for the language to seize the grit of the real. Still, it is not simply a matter of the intrinsic nature of the language. The disparity may be lesser or greater depending on how the language is used. While many French poets were writing in classic verse forms, using only the acceptable "noble" words, Molière was writing of *"clystères,"* enemas, in *Le Malade Imaginaire*. The prose of Stendhal, for example, captures much of the upright straightforwardness of English. *"Va-t'en, maudite tache! va-t'en! dis-je"* doesn't fall far short, if at all, of Lady Macbeth's "Out, damned spot, out, I say!" in its bluntness and the force of its consonants. In his essays decrying the quality of translations of Shakespeare into French, Bonnefoy does not credit the degree of fidelity he achieves in his own Shakespeare translations. The French are often surprised to learn that English has far more words than French. This may be because the French use their language more richly in their daily lives than most English-speakers use theirs. It is a centerpiece of their identity.

Gertrude Stein writes in *Paris France* that "French is a spoken language English really is not." As illustration, she points out that in France, "whenever anybody writes anything and wants anybody to know what it is like they read it out loud. If it is in English it is natural to pass the manuscript to them and let them read it but if it is in french*(sic)* it is natural to read it out loud." Her assessment would seem to be at least partly corroborated by Georges Galichet, who notes in *Physiologie de la Langue*

Française that the phonic element in French is not merely the clothing of the language, it is its body—a lovely image. This would suggest that sound is essential to a French person's experience of the language. On the other hand, a more cynical observer might propose that the French writer reads his manuscript aloud because the French are more natural performers.

Whichever is the case, there is no denying that French is also, of necessity, a written language. Singulars and plurals, for example, verb tenses, agreements between subject and verb, noun and adjective, are not always audible to the ear. Because of the large number of homonyms, context is important in understanding spoken French. It is left to *l'orthographe,* spelling, to differentiate words that sound alike—think of *pain,* bread, *pin,* pine, *peint,* painted. Evidence of the potential ambiguity in spoken French can be seen in the word games called *holorimes,* two-line poems in which the sounds of each line are the same, but the words making up those sounds are different. Some practitioners, including Jean Goudezki, have produced entire sonnets. Goudezki's *"Invitation,"* said to be the world's first *sonnet holorime,* appeared in *Le Chat Noir,* in August 1892. Often lost to the ear in spoken French is the beautiful visual network of grammatical and syntactical connections that one sees in a written text. It is not for nothing that the French are *passionnés de dictées*—dictation fanatics. Students in French schools know well those minutes during the school day in which, as a means to test their skill in spelling and grammar, they are asked to write down passages that the teacher reads to them. I remember my own French teacher, Madame McAllister, doing the same in my French classes. But that's not the end of it. For nineteen years, until ending the program in 2005, culture maven and bibliomane Bernard Pivot presented televised *dictées* for adults that tested even serious linguists.

CONNECTIONS

French is a language that likes things spelled out—in the accords between noun and adjective, subject and verb, object and past participle. Galichet speaks of the "solidarity" between the noun and the adjective that modifies it, of how gender accords illuminate syntactical connections. I like to imagine myself sometimes walking through the forest of connections that make up a passage of prose, deferring to nouns and adjectives standing side by side, searching for the object that gives the past participle its feminine ending, greeting the solitary adverb that remains independent, invariable. French also wants relations to be explicit. In English this is less often the case. An English-speaker will say "toothbrush," for example, but a French person needs to spell it out: *"brosse à dents."* When I spoke earlier of the Promenade Plantée, I called it an example of "industrial reuse." But the term is ambiguous. What does the word "industrial" refer to, the original nature of the site or the kind of reuse? The French take a longer time to express the same idea in the also slightly grandiose *réutilisation* (or *réhabilitation) du patrimoine industriel.* But the relationships are clearer. This tendency to lay things out accounts in large part for French being called a language of reason. But it can lead to laborious extremes. *"Dans le sens des aiguilles d'une montre,"* for example, becomes in English simply "clockwise."

It was several years ago that Bob's house burned to the ground, damaging or completely incinerating almost two thousand of my books. As I made my way through their charred remains, some of them still drenched with the fire fighters' water, I found myself drawn most of all to my books in French. It was they I retrieved first, turning them over in my hands, opening them gently so as not to break already weakened spines. I thought of them almost as talismans, calling me back to my first moment of discovery. But the French books represented only a handful of the total. In the end, with Bob's help, I threw most of the books into a Dumpster he had hired to get rid of the insulation and other nonflammable residue from the house. I just didn't know what else to do. I think I felt, as I hurled each volume upward, something akin to what one would feel if he were throwing someone's ashes into the sea—a spiritually wrenching but richly ceremonial release. Almost all of the French books were salvageable to some degree, along with a small number of books in English. They are now shelved, still smudged with charcoal, some slightly warped, in the dining room of the Pittsburgh apartment. What I will always regret is my decision to throw the set of Shakespeare's plays, individual hardbound volumes, into the Dumpster. They had been grievously damaged, and I thought them replaceable. But this has proven not to be so. At least not in kind. I should have kept them in a box, singed and twisted as they were.

When you speak another language, you go into another place—into a different visual, auditory, and structural network. Looking out my dining-room window, I imagine a blanket of French, silvery, gossamer, descending onto the landscape of Pittsburgh, covering the skyscrapers, the rivers and bridges, the houses clustered on the hills. I cannot visualize English in this way. Nor can I analyze the reasons for the effect English has on me, as I have tried to do with French, with why French speaks to me as it does. I can't really step back from English. In a profile in *The New Yorker* of the Romanian/French writer E. M. Cioran, Adam Gopnik writes that "we breathe in our first language, and swim in our second." In *Les Mots Anglais,* Stéphane Mallarmé writes that the French must leave the task of creating English words to the English themselves; the French can analyze them. This is because, he says, *on ne voit presque jamais si sûrement un mot que de dehors, où nous sommes; c'est-à-dire de l'étranger*—one almost never sees a word so clearly as he does from the outside, where we are; that is, from a foreign land. What is important to me is that French gives me another horizon, another sensibility, an almost physical refuge. When I bought my Paris apartment, I wasn't sure what that presence in Paris would mean to me. But now I know that, as a focal point for my love of the language, it is a haven I carry with me. Whenever I speak or read French, I am in Paris, regardless of where I actually am. The apartment, the forms and shapes of Paris, are a complement to my American self that rounds out my sense of the wholeness of my life, a place in which reality and dream converge, and a place that gives incalculable richness to the joy of words.

Notes

Pages 59-60: Some of the details on page 59 and the top of page 60 were gleaned from *Walks in Gertrude Stein's Paris,* by Mary Ellen Jordan Haight, Salt Lake City: Gibbs M. Smith, 1988.

Page 88: L'anesthésie-réanimation is a branch of medicine in France dedicated to anesthesia and to intensive care, especially of patients who are in life-threatening situations. The doctor who practices this medical specialty is called *un anesthésiste,* or increasingly, *anesthésiologiste,* that is, anesthesiologist.

Page 100: I first encountered the names of some of the St-Sulpice bells in *La Lutte avec l'Ange,* by Jean-Paul Kauffmann. I subsequently wrote to the church to ask whether those were the names of the bells I would have heard on a Sunday morning. Here, translated, is the information I received in reply:

> In fact, we have five bells—the great bell and four others.

NOTES

The first, the great bell, is named Thérèse and weighs 12,012 pounds; cast 1824 by Osmond Dubois and consecrated November 26, 1824 by Monseigneur de Quélen, archbishop of Paris. This bell rings only on special occasions like Easter.

The three that you hear on Sunday are named:
Caroline, cast 1824 by Osmond Dubois, weight 8,060 pounds, consecrated by Monseigneur de Quélen, archbishop of Paris, November 26, 1824;
Louise, cast 1828 by Osmond, weight 6,000 pounds and consecrated by M. de Pierre, priest of Saint Sulpice parish, May 28, 1828;
Marie, cast 1828 by Osmond, weight 5,000 pounds and consecrated by M. de Pierre, priest of Saint Sulpice parish, May 28, 1828.

The fifth, the angelus, is named Henriette Louise, cast 1824 by Osmond Dubois, weight 1,950 pounds and consecrated by Monseigneur de Quélen, archbishop of Paris, November 26, 1824. It rings only twice a day, at noon and 6:30 p.m.

I also asked if the church still had a bell-ringer. The answer is that there is no longer a bell-ringer, but the sacristan goes to a control board to turn on the machinery that makes the bells ring.

Page 120: For the translation of the phrase from *Lire* and for more on Michel Dansel/Thaler, see "All Talk, No Action: A Funeral for Verbs, With Few Pallbearers," *Wall Street Journal,* July 16, 2004, p. 1.

Page 126: Scholars have long debated how much of the itinerary he wrote about Chateaubriand actually accomplished in the new world. Suffice it to say that much of Chateaubriand's writing on America is an amalgam of impressions derived from his own experience as well as the works of other travelers that aspires to a poetic rather than a literal truth.

Page 135: Other favorite magical words: *soupirant,* suitor, from the verb *soupir,* to sigh (I can just see the fellow leaning, sighing over his beloved, hands on heart); *casse-tête,* puzzle, literally head-breaker; *pourboire,* tip, from *pour,* for, and *boire,* to drink; *couvre-pied(s),* literally cover the feet, for a small blanket or quilt at the foot of the bed (I love the snugness of those warm feet under the covers). Then there is the expression *rebrousser chemin,* to turn back, retrace one's steps, from *chemin,* road, way, and *rebrousser,* brush the wrong way, e.g., a cat's fur. The expression vividly evokes one's feet brushing back against their previous forward progress along the path. The image contained in one term may be even too intimate, not to say off-putting: *lèche-vitrine,* window-shopping, literally "licking the windows."

Bibliography

ASSELIN, GILLES AND MASTRON, RUTH, *Au Contraire! Figuring Out the French,* Yarmouth, ME and London: Intercultural Press, 2001.

BALDWIN, JAMES, *Giovanni's Room,* NEW YORK: Doubleday, 1956; reprint Dell Publishing, 2000.

BARZUN, JACQUES, *An Essay on French Verse: For Readers of English Poetry,* New York: New Directions Books, 1991.

BAUDELAIRE, CHARLES, *Les fleurs du mal,* introduction and notes by Antoine Adam, Paris : Éditions Garnier Frères, 1961.

BONNEFOY, YVES, *Shakespeare & the French Poet,* ed. John Naughton, Chicago and London: The University of Chicago Press, 2004.

BOSANQUET, THEODORA, *Paul Valéry,* London: The Hogarth Press, 1933.

BOURGUIGNON, JEAN-PIERRE, quoted in *"La culture n'est plus générale," Télérama,* No. 2795, August 6, 2003.

CHATEAUBRIAND, FRANÇOIS-RENÉ DE, *Atala René,* Paris: Delmas, 1956.

DAVENPORT, MARCIA, *The Valley of Decision,* New York: Charles Scribner's Sons, 1942; reprint Pittsburgh: University of Pittsburgh Press, 1989.

EIFFEL TOWER OFFICIAL SITE, *La Tour Eiffel, site officiel:* www.tour-eiffel.fr

EWERT, ALFRED, *The French Language,* London: Faber & Faber, 1933; second edition, 1943.

LE FIGARO, on demonstrations, *"La moisson dans les Champs,"* June 25, 1990; *"Les éleveurs montrent leur force,"* August 29, 1990.

GALICHET, GEORGES, *Physiologie de la langue française,* Paris: Presses Universitaires de France, 1964.

GOPNIK, ADAM, "The Get-Ready Man," *The New Yorker,* June 19 & 26, 2000.

HEMINGWAY, ERNEST, *The Old Man and the Sea, Le vieil homme et la mer,* bilingual edition, Paris: Gallimard, 2002.

HILLAIRET, JACQUES, *Dictionnaire historique des rues de Paris,* 10th ed., 2 vols., Paris: Les Éditions de Minuit, 1997.

HUGO, VICTOR, *Hernani,* ed. Gilles Guilleron, Paris: Petits Classiques Larousse, 1999.

KAUFFMANN, JEAN-PAUL, *La lutte avec l'Ange,* Paris: La Table Ronde, 2001; English edition, *The Struggle with the Angel: Delacroix, Jacob, and the God of Good and Evil,* trans. Patricia Clancy, New York and London: Four Walls Eight Windows, 2001.

MALLARMÉ, STÉPHANE, *Les mots anglais,* in *Oeuvres complètes,* eds. Henri Mondor and G. Jean-Aubry, Paris: Gallimard, 1945.

RACINE, JEAN, *Phèdre,* trans. Ted Hughes, New York: Farrar, Straus and Giroux, 1998.

RACINE, JEAN, *Phaedra,* trans. Richard Wilbur, San Diego, New York, London: Harcourt Brace, 1986.

RUSSELL, JOHN, *Paris,* New York: Harry N. Abrams, 1983.

BIBLIOGRAPHY

SAYCE, R.A., *Style in French Prose: A Method of Analysis,* Oxford: The Clarendon Press, 1953.

SHAKESPEARE, WILLIAM, *Hamlet,* trans. Jean-Michel Déprats, bilingual edition, Paris: Gallimard, 2002.

SHAKESPEARE, WILLIAM, Macbeth, trans. F.-V. Hugo, rev. Yves Florenne and Élisabeth Duret, Paris: Le Livre de Poche, 1984.

SHAKESPEARE, WILLIAM, *The Tragedy of King Richard the Second,* ed. Robert T. Petersson, New Haven: Yale University Press, 1957.

SHAKESPEARE, WILLIAM, *La Tragédie du roi Richard II,* trans. Jean-Michel Déprats, bilingual edition, Paris: Gallimard, 1998.

STEIN, GERTRUDE, *Paris France,* New York, London: Liveright, 1970 (originally published 1940).

THALER, MICHEL (Michel Dansel), *Le train de nulle part,* Aix-en-Provence: ADCAN Édition, 2004.

VOLKOFF, VLADIMIR, *"La langue française pour un écrivain,"* lecture in the salons of the Sénat, June 21, 2004: reprinted in *Défense de la langue française,* No. 213, July-August-September, 2004, which can be found at www.langue-française.org.